MARQUEE SERIES

MICROSOFT®
ACCESS 2003

EMCParadigm
PUBLISHING

NITA RUTKOSKY
Pierce College at Puyallup – Puyallup, Washington

DENISE SEGUIN
Fanshawe College – London, Ontario

CONTENTS

The Marquee Series Team: Desiree Faulkner, Developmental Editor; Leslie Anderson, Senior Designer; Jennifer Wreisner, Cover Designer; Leslie Anderson, Erica Tava, Desktop Production; Teri Linander, Tester; Sharon O'Donnell, Copyeditor; Lynn Reichel, Proofreader; and Nancy Fulton, Indexer.

Publishing Team: George Provol, Publisher; Janice Johnson, Director of Product Development; Tony Galvin, Acquisitions Editor; Lori Landwer, Marketing Manager; Shelley Clubb, Electronic Design and Production Manager.

Acknowledgment: The authors and publisher wish to thank the following reviewer for her technical and academic assistance in testing exercises and assessing instruction: Susan Lynn Bowen, Valdosta Technical College, Valdosta, GA.

Library of Congress Cataloging-in-Publication Data
 Rutkosky, Nita Hewitt.
 Microsoft Access 2003 / Nita Rutkosky, Denise Seguin.
  p.cm. – (Marquee series)
 Includes index.
 ISBN 0-7638-2071-7 (text) – ISBN 0-7638-2070-9 (text & CD)
  1. Microsoft Access. 2. Databse management. I. Seguin, Denise. II. Title. III. Series

Text + CD: 0-7638-2070-9
Order Number: 05627

© 2004 by Paradigm Publishing Inc.
 Published by **EMC**Paradigm   (800) 535-6865
 875 Montreal Way   E-mail: educate@emcp.com
 St. Paul, MN 55102   Web site: www.emcp.com

Printed in the United States of America
10 9 8 7 6 5 4 3 2 1

Introducing ACCESS 2003

Interacting with a database occurs more often than we realize as we perform our daily routines. Consider the following activities that you might do today: use a bank machine to withdraw cash from your bank account; stop at the gas station and charge the purchase to your credit card; open a telephone book to look up a telephone number; browse an online catalog to comparison shop for something that you need to buy. In all of these activities you would be accessing and/or updating a database. Any time that you look for something by accessing an organized file system you are probably using a database. Microsoft Access 2003 is the database management system included with Microsoft Office.

A *database management system (DBMS)* is used to design, create, input, maintain, manipulate, sort, and print data. Managing data effectively is a vital business activity since data forms the root of all business transactions. Access is a DBMS that includes a variety of powerful features for defining, editing, and formatting database tables, forms, reports, and queries.

While working in Access, you will produce business documents and manage business data for the following six companies:

 First Choice Travel is a travel center offering a full range of traveling services from booking flights, hotel reservations, and rental cars to offering traveling seminars.

 Marquee Productions is involved in all aspects of creating movies from script writing and development to filming.

 The Waterfront Bistro offers fine dining for lunch and dinner and also offers banquet facilities, a wine cellar, and catering services.

 Performance Threads maintains an inventory of rental costumes and also researches, designs, and sews special-order and custom-made costumes.

 Worldwide Enterprises is a national and international distributor of products for a variety of companies and is the exclusive movie distribution agent for Marquee Productions.

 The mission of the Niagara Peninsula College Theatre Arts Division is to offer a curriculum designed to provide students with a thorough exposure to all aspects of the theatre arts.

Managing Data Using Access 2003

Access is a database management system used to design, create, input, maintain, manipulate, sort, and print data. Managing data effectively is a vital business activity since data forms the root of all business transactions. Access is a powerful database management program that provides a range of features for defining, editing, and formatting database tables, forms, reports, and queries. Interesting Access features and elements that you will learn in each section are described below.

Section 1
Maintaining Data in Access Tables

Begin your Access journey by working with table data in Datasheet view. Learn to find and then edit data, add new records, and delete records. Change the appearance of a datasheet by adjusting column widths, moving columns, sorting, and formatting the datasheet. Compacting, repairing, and backing up databases are important Access tools you will also learn in Section 1.

US Distributors Table Datasheet in Topics 1.2 – 1.8

US Distributors   5/10/2003

State	City	Name	Street Address1	Street Address2	Zip Code	Telephone	Fax	E-Mail Address
AZ	Phoenix	LaVista Cinemas	111 Vista Road		86355-6014	602-555-6231	602-555-6233	lavista@emcp.net
CA	Los Angeles	Marquee Movies	1011 South Alameda Street		90045	612-555-2398	612-555-2377	marqueemovies@emcp.net
FL	Tampa	Suntest Cinemas		341 South Fourth Avenue	33562	813-555-3185	813-555-3177	suntest@emcp.net
GA	Atlanta	Liberty Cinemas	P. O. Box 998	12011 Ruston Way	73125	404-555-8113	404-555-2349	libertycinemas@emcp.net
IL	Oak Park	O'Shea Movies	59 Erie		60302	312-555-7719	312-555-7381	oshea@emcp.net
KS	Emporia	Midtown Moviehouse	1033 Commercial Street		66801	316-555-7013	316-555-7022	midtown@emcp.net
KY	Louisville	All Nite Cinemas	2188 3rd Street		40201	502-555-4238	502-555-4240	allnite@emcp.net
MA	Cambridge	Eastown Movie House	P. O. Box 429	1 Concourse Avenue	02142	413-555-0981	413-555-0226	eastown@emcp.net
MD	Baltimore	Dockside Movies	P. O. Box 224	155 S. Central Avenue	21203	301-555-7732	301-555-9836	dockside@emcp.net
MI	Detroit	Renaissance Cinemas	3599 Woodward Avenue		48211	313-555-1693	313-555-1699	renaissance-cinemas@emcp.net
NJ	Baking Ridge	Hillman Cinemas	55 Kemble Avenue		07920	201-555-1147	201-555-1143	hillman@emcp.net
NY	Buffalo	Waterfront Cinemas	P. O. Box 3255		14288	716-555-3845	716-555-4860	waterfrontcinemas@emcp.net
NY	New York	Cinema Festival	318 East 11th Street		10003	212-555-9715	212-555-9717	cinemafestival@emcp.net
NY	New York	Movie Emporium	203 West Houston Street		10014	212-555-7278	212-555-7280	movie-emporium@emcp.net
NY	New York	Westview Movies	1112 Broadway		10119	212-555-4875	212-555-4877	westview@emcp.net
OH	Dublin	Mooretown Movies	P. O. Box 11	331 Metro Place	43107	614-555-8134	614-555-8339	mooretown@emcp.net
OR	Portland	Redwood Cinemas	P. O. Box 112F	336 Ninth Street	97466-3359	503-555-8641	503-555-8633	redwoodcinemas@emcp.net
PA	Philadelphia	Wellington 10	1203 Tenth Southwest		19178	215-555-9045	215-555-9048	wellington10@emcp.net
SC	Columbia	Danforth Cinemas	P. O. Box 22	18 Pickens Street	29201	803-555-3487	803-555-3421	danforth@emcp.net
TX	Arlington	Century Cinemas	3687 Avenue K		76013	817-555-2116	817-555-2119	centurycinemas@emcp.net
WA	Seattle	Mainstream Movies	P. O. Box 33	333 Evergreen Building	98220-2791	206-555-3269	206-555-3270	mainstream@emcp.net

Dashed line is used to show that the printout requires two pages.

US Distributors Table Datasheet in Topic 1.9

US Distributors   5/11/2003

State	City	Name	Street Address1	Street Address2	Zip Code	Telephone	Fax	E-Mail Address
AZ	Phoenix	LaVista Cinemas	111 Vista Road		86355-6014	602-555-6231	602-555-6233	lavista@emcp.net
CA	Los Angeles	Marquee Movies	1011 South Alameda Street		90045	612-555-2398	612-555-2377	marqueemovies@emcp.net
FL	Tampa	Suntest Cinemas		341 South Fourth Avenue	33562	813-555-3185	813-555-3177	suntest@emcp.net
GA	Atlanta	Liberty Cinemas	P. O. Box 998	12011 Ruston Way	73125	404-555-8113	404-555-2349	libertycinemas@emcp.net
IL	Oak Park	O'Shea Movies	59 Erie		60302	312-555-7719	312-555-7381	oshea@emcp.net
KS	Emporia	Midtown Moviehouse	1033 Commercial Street		66801	316-555-7013	316-555-7022	midtown@emcp.net
KY	Louisville	All Nite Cinemas	2188 3rd Street		40201	502-555-4238	502-555-4240	allnite@emcp.net
MA	Cambridge	Eastown Movie House	P. O. Box 429	1 Concourse Avenue	02142	413-555-0981	413-555-0226	eastown@emcp.net
MD	Baltimore	Dockside Movies	P. O. Box 224	155 S. Central Avenue	21203	301-555-7732	301-555-9836	dockside@emcp.net
MI	Detroit	Renaissance Cinemas	3599 Woodward			313-555-1693	313-555-1699	renaissance-cinemas@emcp.net
NJ	Baking Ridge	Hillman Cinemas	55 Kemble A			201-555-1147	201-555-1143	hillman@emcp.net
NY	Buffalo	Waterfront Cinemas	P. O. Box 325			716-555-3845	716-555-4860	waterfrontcinemas@emcp.net
NY	New York	Cinema Festival	318 East 11th			212-555-9715	212-555-9717	cinemafestival@emcp.net
NY	New York	Movie Emporium	203 West Ho			212-555-7278	212-555-7280	movie-emporium@emcp.net
NY	New York	Westview Movies	1112 Broadway		10119	212-555-4875	212-555-4877	westview@emcp.net
OH	Dublin	Mooretown Movies	P. O. Box 11	331 Metro Place	43107	614-555-8134	614-555-8339	mooretown@emcp.net
OR	Portland	Redwood Cinemas	P. O. Box 112F	336 Ninth Street	97466-3359	503-555-8641	503-555-8633	redwoodcinemas@emcp.net
PA	Philadelphia	Wellington 10	1203 Tenth Southwest		19178	215-555-9045	215-555-9048	wellington10@emcp.net
SC	Columbia	Danforth Cinemas	P. O. Box 22	18 Pickens Street	29201	803-555-3487	803-555-3421	danforth@emcp.net
TX	Arlington	Century Cinemas	3687 Avenue K		76013	817-555-2116	817-555-2119	centurycinemas@emcp.net
WA	Seattle	Mainstream Movies	P. O. Box 33	333 Evergreen Building	98220-2791	206-555-3269	206-555-3270	mainstream@emcp.net

An adjusted row height creates more space between records. Added space makes the printout easier to read.

Section 2

Creating Tables and Relationships

After you have mastered the basic terminology and navigated a table in datasheet view, you are ready to learn how to create tables. The ability to create a relationship between tables is one of the most powerful Access features, allowing the user to extract data from multiple tables as if they were one.

Employee Benefits Table Created in Topics 2.1 – 2.5

A validation rule created for the *Life Insurance* field prevents users from entering values greater than $200,000.

A restricted drop-down list for the *Vacation* field is used to enter the number of vacation weeks.

Employee Benefits

Emp No	Pension Plan	Dental Plan	Premium Health	Dependents	Life Insurance	Pension Eligibility	Vacation
1001	☑	☐	☑	2	$150,000.00	22-Jan-99	4 weeks
1005	☑	☑	☑	3	$175,000.00	15-Feb-99	3 weeks
1010	☑	☐	☐	0	$100,000.00	30-Jul-99	
1015	☑	☑	☑	2	$199,999.00		
1020	☑	☐	☐	0	$100,000.00		

The *Pension Eligibility* field has an input mask and is formatted to *Medium Date*.

Employees Table Created in Topics 2.6 – 2.7

	Employees						5/25/2003
Employee Number	First Name	Middle Name	Last Name	Address	City	State/Province	Postal Code
1001	Sam	Lawrence	Vestering	287-1501 Broadway	New York	NY	10110

Employees table created using Table Wizard. The datasheet is formatted to add a background and gridline color and display in a different font and font size.

Relationships Report in Topic 2.8

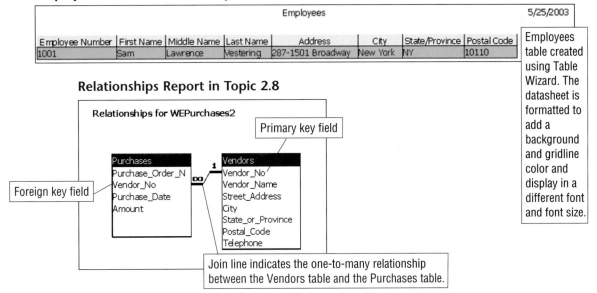

Relationships for WEPurchases2

Primary key field

Foreign key field

Purchases
Purchase_Order_N
Vendor_No
Purchase_Date
Amount

Vendors
Vendor_No
Vendor_Name
Street_Address
City
State_or_Province
Postal_Code
Telephone

Join line indicates the one-to-many relationship between the Vendors table and the Purchases table.

Relationships Report in Topic 2.9

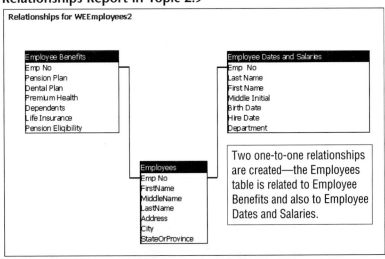

Relationships for WEEmployees2

Employee Benefits
Emp No
Pension Plan
Dental Plan
Premium Health
Dependents
Life Insurance
Pension Eligibility

Employee Dates and Salaries
Emp No
Last Name
First Name
Middle Initial
Birth Date
Hire Date
Department

Employees
Emp No
FirstName
MiddleName
LastName
Address
City
StateOrProvince

Two one-to-one relationships are created—the Employees table is related to Employee Benefits and also to Employee Dates and Salaries.

Section 3
Creating Queries, Forms, and Reports

In section 3 you learn how to extract specific information from tables using a query. Forms provide a more user-friendly interface for entering, editing, and deleting records. Create a report when you need to control the layout of data on the page and include rich text formatting options.

Query Showing Employees with Either 3 or 4 Weeks Vacation in Topic 3.3

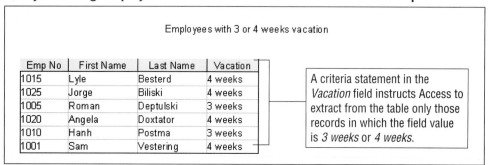

Employees with 3 or 4 weeks vacation

Emp No	First Name	Last Name	Vacation
1015	Lyle	Besterd	4 weeks
1025	Jorge	Biliski	4 weeks
1005	Roman	Deptulski	3 weeks
1020	Angela	Doxtator	4 weeks
1010	Hanh	Postma	3 weeks
1001	Sam	Vestering	4 weeks

A criteria statement in the *Vacation* field instructs Access to extract from the table only those records in which the field value is *3 weeks* or *4 weeks*.

Performing Calculations in a Query in Topic 3.4

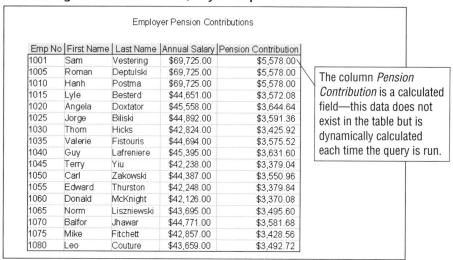

Employer Pension Contributions

Emp No	First Name	Last Name	Annual Salary	Pension Contribution
1001	Sam	Vestering	$69,725.00	$5,578.00
1005	Roman	Deptulski	$69,725.00	$5,578.00
1010	Hanh	Postma	$69,725.00	$5,578.00
1015	Lyle	Besterd	$44,651.00	$3,572.08
1020	Angela	Doxtator	$45,558.00	$3,644.64
1025	Jorge	Biliski	$44,892.00	$3,591.36
1030	Thom	Hicks	$42,824.00	$3,425.92
1035	Valerie	Fistouris	$44,694.00	$3,575.52
1040	Guy	Lafreniere	$45,395.00	$3,631.60
1045	Terry	Yiu	$42,238.00	$3,379.04
1050	Carl	Zakowski	$44,387.00	$3,550.96
1055	Edward	Thurston	$42,248.00	$3,379.84
1060	Donald	McKnight	$42,126.00	$3,370.08
1065	Norm	Liszniewski	$43,695.00	$3,495.60
1070	Balfor	Jhawar	$44,771.00	$3,581.68
1075	Mike	Fitchett	$42,857.00	$3,428.56
1080	Leo	Couture	$43,659.00	$3,492.72

The column *Pension Contribution* is a calculated field—this data does not exist in the table but is dynamically calculated each time the query is run.

Salary Statistics Calculated Using Aggregate Functions in Topic 3.5

Annual Salary Statistics

Total Annual Salaries	Average Annual Salary	Maximum Annual Salary	Minimum Annual Salary
$823,170.00	$48,421.76	$69,725.00	$42,126.00

Access includes aggregate functions that are used to calculate statistics on table data.

Salary Statistics Grouped by Department in Topic 3.5

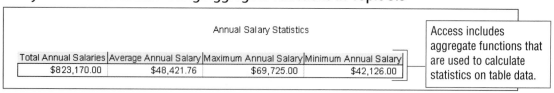

Annual Salary Statistics by Department

Total Annual Salaries	Average Annual Salary	Maximum Annual Salary	Minimum Annual Salary	Department
$286,829.00	$47,804.83	$69,725.00	$42,126.00	European Distribution
$248,521.00	$49,704.20	$69,725.00	$43,695.00	North American Distribution
$287,820.00	$47,970.00	$69,725.00	$42,248.00	Overseas Distribution

Aggregate functions grouped by the *Department* field.

ACCESS

Employee Dates and Salaries Form Created in Topics 3.6 – 3.7

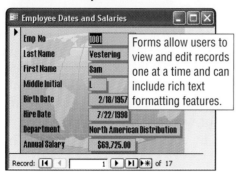

Forms allow users to view and edit records one at a time and can include rich text formatting features.

Employee Benefits and Employees Form with Label Objects Added in Topic 3.8

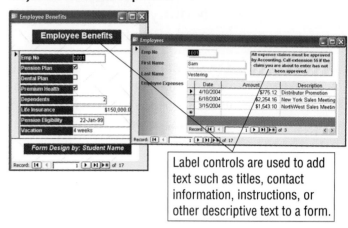

Label controls are used to add text such as titles, contact information, instructions, or other descriptive text to a form.

Employee Mailing Addresses Report Created in Topics 3.9 – 3.10

Create a report when you want to specify which fields to print and to have more control over the report layout and format.

Employee Mailing Addresses

Last Name	Besterd	City	New York
First Name	Lyle	State/Province	NY
Address	1258 Park Avenue	Postal Code	10110-

Last Name	Biliski	City	New York
First Name	Jorge	State/Province	NY
Address	439 7th Avenue	Postal Code	10111-

Last Name	Couture	City	New York
First Name	Leo	State/Province	NY
Address	908-1200 W 46th St.	Postal Code	10110-

Last Name	Deptulski	City	New York
First Name	Roman	State/Province	NY
Address	112-657 E 39th St.	Postal Code	10111-

Last Name	Doxtator	City	New York
First Name	Angela	State/Province	NY
Address	201-654 W 50th St.	Postal Code	10110-

Last Name	Fistouris	City	New York
First Name	Valerie	State/Province	NY
Address	210 York Avenue	Postal Code	10111-

Last Name	Fitchett	City	New York
First Name	Mike	State/Province	NY
Address	329-1009 W 23rd St.	Postal Code	10111-

Last Name	Hicks	City	New York
First Name	Thom	State/Province	NY
Address	329-5673 W 63rd St.	Postal Code	10111-

Section 4
Modifying Tables and Reports, Performing Calculations, and Viewing Data

The structure of a table is modified by inserting, deleting, and moving fields. Access provides many methods with which you can view data such as filtering; summarizing using a crosstab query, a PivotTable, or a PivotChart; finding duplicate or finding unmatched records; and data access pages for working in a database on the Web. Calculations are added to forms and reports by entering a formula in a text box control object.

Modified Employee Dates and Salaries Table in Topic 4.1

Employee Dates and Salaries : Table

	Emp	Birth Date	Annual Salary	Hire Date	Review Date	Department
▶ +	1001	2/18/1957	$69,725.00	7/22/1998		North American Distribution
+	1005	3/12/1948	$69,725.00	8/15/1998		Overseas Distribution
+	1010	12/10/1952	$69,725.00	1/30/1999		European Distribution
+	1015	10/15/1959	$45,651.00	5/17/1999		North American Distribution
+	1020	5/22/1963	$45,558.00	8/3/		nerican Distribution
+	1025	6/18/1970	$44,892.00	12/1/		nerican Distribution
+	1030	7/27/1977	$42,824.00	1/22/		s Distribution
+	1035	2/4/1970	$44,694.00	3/15/		n Distribution
+	1040	9/14/1972	$45,395.00	3/10/		s Distribution
+	1045	6/18/1961	$42,238.00	4/12/		n Distribution
+	1050	5/9/1967	$44,387.00	2/9/		n Distribution
+	1055	1/3/1960	$42,248.00	6/22/2002		Overseas Distribution
+	1060	1/6/1964	$42,126.00	6/22/2003		European Distribution
+	1065	11/16/1970	$43,695.00	2/6/2003		North American Distribution
+	1070	9/3/1973	$44,771.00	11/22/2004		Overseas Distribution
+	1075	4/18/1966	$42,857.00	3/19/2004		Overseas Distribution
+	1080	1/8/1978	$43,659.00	1/17/2004		European Distribution
*			$0.00			

Modified table structure with new field *(Review Date)* inserted and moved *Annual Salary* field.

Modifying Forms and Reports in Topics 4.6 – 4.7

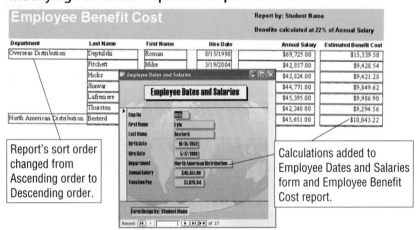

Report's sort order changed from Ascending order to Descending order.

Calculations added to Employee Dates and Salaries form and Employee Benefit Cost report.

Data Access Page Created in Topic 4.10

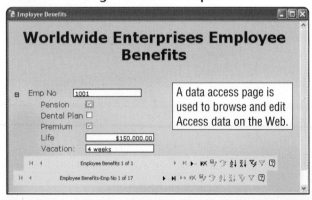

A data access page is used to browse and edit Access data on the Web.

ACCESS SECTION 1

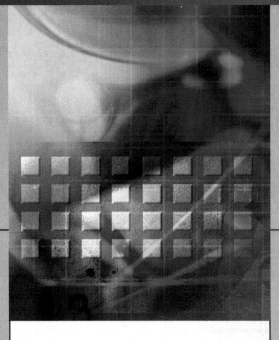

Maintaining Data in Access Tables

Managing business information effectively is a vital activity, since data forms the basis upon which transactions are conducted or strategic decisions are made. Microsoft Office Access 2003 is a database management system that is used to store, retrieve, and manage information. The type of information stored in an Access database can include such items as customer lists, inventory articles, human resources, and supplier lists. Activities that are routinely performed with a database include adding, editing, deleting, finding, sorting, querying, and reporting information. In this section you will learn the skills and complete the projects described here.

Note: The database files for this section are in the AccessS1 subfolder in the Access folder on the CD that accompanies this textbook. Because the database files are large and will increase in size as you work with them, do not copy the entire subfolder to a floppy disk. You will copy each database as it is used in the text and then remove the read-only attribute from the database file on your disk so that you can make changes to the database file. To remove the read-only attribute:

1. *Copy the database file from the CD to your disk.*
2. *In Access, display the Open dialog box with the drive active containing your disk.*
3. *Click once on the database file name.*
4. *Click the Tools button on the Open dialog box toolbar and then click Properties at the drop-down list.*
5. *At the Properties dialog box with the General tab selected, click Read-only in the Attributes section to remove the check mark.*
6. *Click OK to close the Properties dialog box.*
7. *Open the database file.*

Skills

- Define *field, record, table, datasheet,* and *database*
- Start and exit Access
- Identify features in the Access window
- Open and close a database
- Open and close tables
- Adjust column widths
- Navigate in Datasheet view
- Find and edit records
- Add records
- Delete records
- Sort records
- Move columns in Datasheet view
- Preview and print a table
- Change the page orientation
- Change the row height of records in a datasheet
- Use the Help feature
- Compact and repair a database
- Back up a database

Projects

Add, delete, find, and sort records; preview, change page orientation, margins, and print tables; increase row height; compact and back up the Distributors database; find, edit, add, delete, and sort records; preview, change page setup and print; compact and back up the Employees database.

Find student records and input grades into the Grades database; compact and back up the Grades database.

Maintain the Inventory database by adding and deleting records; compact the inventory database.

Delete records, sort, increase row height, and print two reports from the Costume Inventory database; compact the inventory database.

1.1 Exploring Database Objects

A *database* contains information logically organized into related units for easy retrieval. You access a database when you open a telephone book to look up a friend's telephone number, or browse the yellow pages looking for a restaurant. Microsoft Office Access 2003 is an application that is used to manage databases electronically. Information stored in an Access database is organized into *tables*. A

table contains information for related items such as customers, suppliers, inventory, or human resources.

PROJECT: You will open and close two tables and a form in the Distributors database for Worldwide Enterprises to define and identify objects, fields, records, tables, datasheets, and forms.

S T E P S

1. At the Windows desktop, click the Start button ⊞ start on the Taskbar.

2. Point to All Programs.

3. Point to Microsoft Office.

4. Click Microsoft Office Access 2003.

    Depending on your operating system and/or system configuration, the steps you complete to open Access may vary.

5. Click the Open button 📂 on the Database toolbar or click the <u>More</u> hyperlink in the *Open* section of the Getting Started task pane.

    Refer to the Section 1 opening page for instructions on copying a database file from the CD that accompanies this textbook. These steps will have to be repeated for every database.

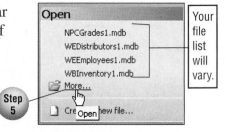

6. If necessary, change to the location where the student data files are located. To change to a different drive, click the down-pointing arrow to the right of the *Look in* option box and then select the correct drive from the drop-down list.

7. Double-click *WEDistributors1.mdb*. (*Note: Click Yes to confirm that you want to open the file if a Security warning message box appears stating that unsafe expressions are not blocked. This message may or may not appear depending on the security level setting on the computer you are using. If the message appears, expect that it will reappear each time you open a database file.*)

    Access databases end with the file name extension *mdb*.

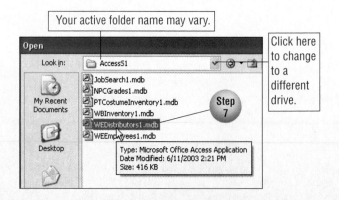

FIGURE A1.1 The Access Screen

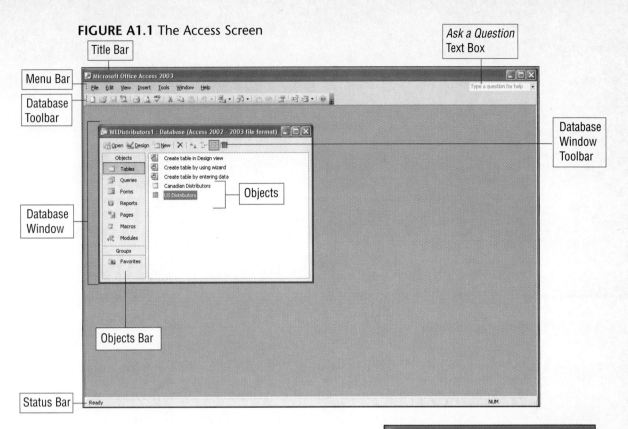

At the top: Title Bar, *Ask a Question Text Box*

Left labels: Menu Bar, Database Toolbar, Database Window, Objects Bar, Status Bar

Right labels: Database Window Toolbar

Center label: Objects

Step 9

8. At the Access screen, identify the various features by comparing your screen with the one shown in Figure A1.1.

   Unlike other Microsoft Office applications, only one database can be open at a time. A database is comprised of a series of objects. Descriptions of the seven types of objects that can be stored in a database are presented in Table A1.1 on page 5. An open database file displays in a Database window that contains the names of the various objects.

9. With Tables the default object selected on the Objects bar, double-click *Canadian Distributors*.

   Canadian Distributors is one of two tables stored within the database. Double-clicking the object named *Canadian Distributors* opens the table in Datasheet view. Datasheets display the contents of a table in a column/row format.

10. Compare your screen with the one shown in Figure A1.2 on page 4 and examine the identified elements.

    The identified elements are further described in Table A1.2 on page 5.

11. Identify the fields and the field names in the Canadian Distributors table. Notice each field contains only one unit of information.

    The field names *Name, Street Address1, Street Address2,* and so on are displayed in the gray header row in Datasheet view.

12. Identify the records in the Canadian Distributors table. Each record is one row in the table.

    The right-pointing arrow in the gray column (called the Record Selector bar) to the left of *EastCoast Cinemas* in Figure A1.2 illustrates the active record.

(continued)

FIGURE A1.2 Canadian Distributors Datasheet

Each column represents a field in the table.

Table Name

Each row is one record in the table.

Record Navigation Bar

Field Names

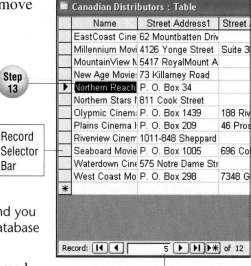

13) Press the Down Arrow key four times to move the active record.

The right-pointing arrow moves down the Record Selector bar as you move the insertion point and the record number at the bottom of the window changes to indicate you are viewing record 5 of a total of 12 records.

Step 13

Record Selector Bar

14) Click the Close button ✕ at the right edge of the Canadian Distributors Table title bar.

The Canadian Distributors table closes and you are returned to the WEDistributors1 : Database window.

Record number changes as you move to a new record.

15) Move the mouse pointer over the table named *US Distributors* and then click the mouse to select the object.

16) Click Open on the Database window toolbar.

Step 16

The US Distributors table opens in Datasheet view.

17) Review the fields and records in the US Distributors datasheet and then click the Close button on the US Distributors Table title bar.

Step 18

18) Click the Forms button on the Objects bar.

19) Double-click *US Distributors*.

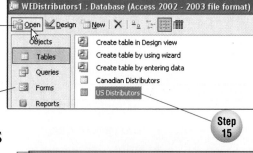

Step 15

The US Distributors form opens in Form view. A form is used to view and edit data in a table one record at a time. Use buttons on the Record Navigation bar to scroll the records.

Step 19

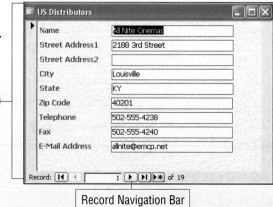

Record Navigation Bar

⑳ Click the Close button on the US Distributors title bar.

㉑ Click File and then Exit.

TABLE A1.1 Database Objects

Object	Description
Tables	Organize data in fields (columns) and rows (records). A database must contain at least one table. The table is the base upon which other objects are created.
Queries	Used to display data from a table that meets a conditional statement and/or perform calculations. For example, display only those records in which the city is Toronto.
Forms	Allow fields and records to be presented in a different layout than the datasheet. Use to facilitate data entry and maintenance.
Reports	Print data from tables or queries. Calculations can be performed in a report.
Pages	Web pages designed for working with data within a Web browser.
Macros	Automate repetitive tasks.
Modules	Advanced automation through programming using Visual Basic for Applications.

TABLE A1.2 Elements of a Database

Element	Description
Field	A single component of information about a person, place, item, or object
Record	All of the fields for one unit such as a customer, supplier, or inventory item
Table	All of the records for one logical group
Datasheet view	Data for a table displayed in columns (fields) and rows (records)
Database	A file containing related tables

In Addition

Planning and Designing a Database

One of the first steps in designing a table for a new database is to look at the format from which the input will originate. For example, look at an existing file card for a customer to see how the information is currently organized. Determine how you will break down all of the information into fields. Discuss with others what the future needs of the company will be for both input and output. Include fields you anticipate will be used in the future. For example, add a field for a Web site address even if you do not currently have URLs for your customers. Refer to Performance Plus Assessment 5 at the end of this section for an exercise using the steps required to design a new database.

In BRIEF

Start Access
1 Click Start.
2 Point to All Programs.
3 Point to Microsoft Office.
4 Click Microsoft Office Access 2003.

Open Objects
1 Open database file.
2 Select type of object from Objects bar.
3 Double-click object name.

1.2 Adjusting Column Width; Navigating in Datasheet View

A table opened in Datasheet view displays data in a manner similar to a spreadsheet, with a grid of columns and rows. Columns contain the field values, with the field names in the gray column headings row at the top of the datasheet. Records are represented in rows. A gray record selector bar is positioned at the left edge of the window. The Record Navigation bar displays along the bottom of the window with record selector buttons. Horizontal and/or vertical scroll bars appear if the entire table is not visible in the current window.

PROJECT: You will adjust column widths and practice scrolling and navigating through records using the US Distributors table.

STEPS

1. Start Access.

2. Click the WEDistributors1.mdb link in the *Open* section of the Getting Started task pane.

   By default, the last four database files opened are displayed in the *Open* section of the Getting Started task pane. The recently used file list option can be adjusted to include up to the last nine files opened. Display the Options dialog box using the Tools menu and then click the General tab to adjust this setting.

   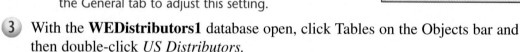

   Step 2

   Open
   WEDistributors1.mdb
   PTCos heInventory1.mdb
   A:\Access51\WEDistributors1.mdb
   WBInventory1.mdb
   More...
   Create a new file...

3. With the **WEDistributors1** database open, click Tables on the Objects bar and then double-click *US Distributors*.

   The US Distributors table opens in Datasheet view.

4. Click the Maximize button ☐ on the US Distributors Table title bar.

   Notice that some columns contain data that is not entirely visible. In Steps 5–7, you will learn how to adjust the column widths using two methods.

   PROBLEM ❓
   If the table window is already maximized, the Maximize button is replaced with the Restore Window ⊡ button. Skip Step 4.

5. With the active record the first row in the table and the insertion point positioned at the left edge of the text in the *Name* field, click Format and then Column Width.

6. Click the Best Fit button in the Column Width dialog box.

   The column is automatically widened to accommodate the width of the longest entry. In the next step you will widen a column using the mouse in the column headings row.

   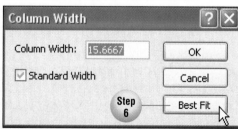

   Column Width

   Column Width: 15.6667   OK

   ☑ Standard Width   Cancel

   Step 6   Best Fit

(7) Position the mouse pointer on the right column boundary line in the Field Name headings row between columns two and three (*Street Address1* and *Street Address2*) until the pointer changes to a vertical line with a left- and right-pointing arrow and then double-click the left mouse button.

Street Address	Street Address2
2188 3rd Street	

Step 7

Step 9

Scroll Box

Step 11

> Double-clicking the column boundary performs the Best Fit command.

(8) Best Fit the *Street Address2* column using either method learned in Steps 5–6 or Step 7.

(9) Click the right-pointing horizontal scroll arrow as many times as necessary to scroll the datasheet to the right and view the remaining columns. (Scrolling can also be performed using keyboard commands, as shown in Table A1.3.)

(10) Best Fit the *E-mail Address* column.

(11) Drag the horizontal scroll box to the left edge of the horizontal scroll bar.

> This scrolls the screen to the left until the first column is visible.

(12) Click the Save button 🖫 on the Database toolbar.

(13) Click the Next Record button ▶ on the Record Navigation bar to move the active record down one row.

(14) Click the Last Record button ▶I on the Record Navigation bar to move the active record to the last row in the table.

(15) Click the Previous Record button ◀ on the Record Navigation bar to move the active record to the second last row in the table.

(16) Click the First Record button I◀ on the Record Navigation bar to move the active record back to the first row in the table.

TABLE A1.3 Scrolling Techniques Using the Keyboard

Press	To Move to
Home	First field in the current record
End	Last field in the current record
Tab	Next field in the current record
Shift + Tab	Previous field in the current record
Ctrl + Home	First field in the first record
Ctrl + End	Last field in the last record

In Addition

Saving Data

Microsoft Access differs from other Office applications in that data is *automatically* saved as soon as you move to the next record or close the table. Database management systems are such a critical component of business activities that saving is not left to chance. The Save button was used in this topic to save the layout changes that were made when the column widths were enlarged.

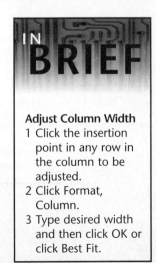

IN BRIEF

Adjust Column Width
1 Click the insertion point in any row in the column to be adjusted.
2 Click Format, Column.
3 Type desired width and then click OK or click Best Fit.

1.3 Finding and Editing Records

The Find command can be used to quickly move the insertion point to a specific record in a table. This is a time-saving feature when the table contains several records that are not all visible in one screen. Once a record has been located, click the insertion point within a field and insert or delete text as required to edit the record.

PROJECT: You have received a note from Sam Vestering that Waterfront Cinemas has changed its fax number and Eastown Movie House has a new P.O. Box number. You will use the Find feature to locate the records and make the changes.

S T E P S

(1) With the US Distributors table open and the insertion point positioned in the *Name* column, click the Find button 🔍 on the Database toolbar.

   This displays the Find and Replace dialog box.

(2) Type **Waterfront Cinemas** in the *Find What* text box and then click the Find Next button.

   The insertion point moves to record 17.

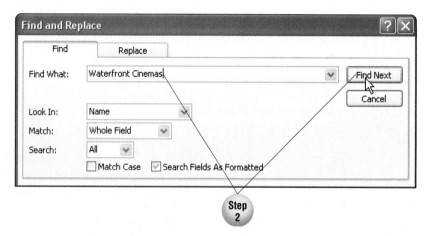

Step 2

(3) Click the Close button on the Find and Replace dialog box title bar.

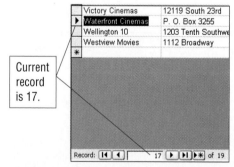

Current record is 17.

(4) Press Tab or Enter seven times to move to the *Fax* column.

   The entire field value is selected when you move from column to column using Tab or Enter. If you need to edit only a few characters within the field you will want to use Edit mode. As an alternative, you could scroll and click the insertion point within the field to avoid having to turn on Edit mode.

(5) Press F2 to turn on Edit mode.

⑥ Press the Left Arrow key four times, delete *3947*, and then type **4860**.

Step 6

619-555-8748	victory@emcp.net
716-555-4860	waterfrontcinemas@
215-555-9048	wellington10@emcp.
212-555-4877	westview@emcp.net

⑦ Look on the record selector bar for record 17 at the pencil icon that is displayed.

> The pencil icon indicates the current record is being edited and the changes have not yet been saved.

Pencil icon indicates record is being edited.

Step 7

	Victory Cinemas
✎	Waterfront Cinemas
	Wellington 10
	Westview Movies

⑧ Press Enter twice to move to the next record in the table.

> The pencil icon disappears, indicating the changes have now been saved.

⑨ Click in any record in the *Street Address1* column and then click the Find button.

⑩ Type **Box 722** in the *Find What* text box.

⑪ Click the down-pointing arrow next to the *Match* list box and then click *Any Part of Field* in the drop-down list.

> Using the options from the *Match* list box you can find records without specifying the entire field value. Specifically, you can instruct Access to stop at records where the entry typed in the *Find What* text box is the *Whole Field* entry; is *Any Part of Field;* or is the *Start of Field.*

⑫ Click Find Next.

> The insertion point moves to record 5. You were able to correctly locate the record for Eastown Movie House using only a portion of the field value for *Street Address1.* Notice Access

Find and Replace — Find | Replace

Find What: Box 722 — Step 10 — Find Next — Cancel
Look In: Street Address1
Match: Whole Field — Step 11
 Any Part of Field
 Whole Field
 Start of Field — earch Fields As Formatted
Search: — Step 12

> has selected *Box 722* in the field—only the text specified in the *Find What* text box (not *P. O. Box 722* which is the entire field value).

⑬ Close the Find and Replace dialog box.

⑭ Press F2 to turn on Edit mode, press Backspace three times, type **429**, and then click in any other record to save the changes to record 5.

In Addition

Using the Replace Command

Use the Replace tab in the Find and Replace dialog box to automatically change a field entry to something else. For example, in Steps 9–12 you searched for *Box 722* and then edited the field to change the box number to *429*. The Replace command could have been used to change the text automatically. To do this, display the Find and Replace dialog box, click the Replace tab, type **Box 722** in the *Find What* text box, type **Box 429** in the Replace With text box, change the option in the *Match* option box to *Any Part of Field,* and then click the Find Next button. Click the Replace button when the record is found. Use the Replace All button in the dialog box to change multiple occurrences of a field.

IN BRIEF

Find a Record
1 Click in any row in the field by which you want to search.
2 Click Edit, Find, or click Find button.
3 Type the search text.
4 Click Find Next.

1.4 Adding Records in Datasheet View

New records can be added to a table in either Datasheet view or Form view. To add a record in Datasheet view, open the table, click the New Record button on either the Table Datasheet toolbar or the Record Navigation bar, and then type the data. Press Tab or Enter to move from field to field. When you press Tab or Enter after typing the last field, the record is automatically saved. Initially, the new record will appear at the bottom of the datasheet until the table is closed. When the table is reopened, the records are rearranged to display alphabetically sorted by the field that has been defined as the primary key. In Addition at the end of this topic describes a primary key field.

PROJECT: Worldwide Enterprises has signed two new distributors in the United States. You will add the information in the US Distributors table.

STEPS

1. With the US Distributors table open, click the New Record button ▶* on the Table Datasheet toolbar.

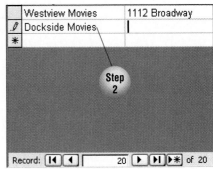

The insertion point moves to the first column in the blank row at the bottom of the datasheet and the record navigation box indicates you are editing record 20.

2. Type **Dockside Movies** and then press Tab.

3. Type **P. O. Box 224** and then press Tab.

4. Type **155 S. Central Avenue** and then press Tab.

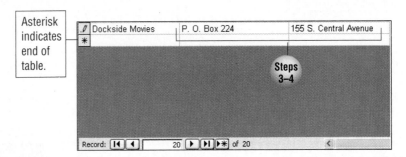

Asterisk indicates end of table.

5. Type **Baltimore** and then press Tab.

6. Type **MD** and then press Tab.

7. Type **21203** and then press Tab.

> **PROBLEM?**
> Press Enter to move to the next field if you are using the numeric keypad to input numbers—it will be more comfortable.

8. Type **301-555-7732** and then press Tab.

9. Type **301-555-9836** and then press Tab.

10. Type **dockside@emcp.net** and then press Tab.

The insertion point moves to a new row when you press Tab or Enter after the last field in a new record to allow you to continue typing the next new record in the table. The record just entered is automatically saved.

⑪ Type the following information in the next row:

Renaissance Cinemas
3599 Woodward
Avenue
Detroit, MI 48211
313-555-1693
313-555-1699
renaissance-
cinemas@emcp.net

⑫ Increase the column width of the *E-Mail Address* column to view all of the data.

⑬ Close the US Distributors table. Click Yes when prompted to save changes to the layout of the table.

⑭ Reopen the US Distributors table to view where the new records are now positioned.

⑮ Close the US Distributors table.

Step 12

State	Zip Code	Telephone	Fax	E-Mail Address
KY	40201	502-555-4238	502-555-4240	allnite@emcp.net
TX	76013	817-555-2116	817-555-2119	centurycinemas@emcp.net
VT	05201	802-555-1469	802-555-1470	countryside@emcp.net
SC	29201	803-555-3487	803-555-3421	danforth@emcp.net
MA	02142	413-555-0981	413-555-0226	eastown@emcp.net
NJ	07920	201-555-1147	201-555-1143	hillman@emcp.net
AZ	86355-6014	602-555-6231	602-555-6233	lavista@emcp.net
GA	73125	404-555-8113	404-555-2349	libertycinemas@emcp.net
WA	98220-2791	206-555-3269	206-555-3270	mainstream@emcp.net
CA	90045	612-555-2398	612-555-2377	marqueemovies@emcp.net
KS	66801	316-555-7013	316-555-7022	midtown@emcp.net
OH	43107	614-555-8134	614-555-8339	mooretown@emcp.net
IL	60302	312-555-7719	312-555-7381	oshea@emcp.net
OR	97466-3359	503-555-8641	503-555-8633	redwoodcinemas@emcp.net
FL	33562	813-555-3185	813-555-3177	sunfest@emcp.net
CA	97432-1567	619-555-8746	619-555-8748	victory@emcp.net
NY	14288	716-555-3845	716-555-4860	waterfrontcinemas@emcp.net
PA	19178	215-555-9045	215-555-9048	wellington10@emcp.net
NY	10119	212-555-4875	212-555-4877	westview@emcp.net
MD	21203	301-555-7732	301-555-9836	dockside@emcp.net
MI	48211	313-555-1693	313-555-1699	renaissance-cinemas@emcp.net

Step 11

New records initially appear at the bottom of the datasheet.

New records have now been rearranged alphabetically by name.

Name	Street Address1
All Nite Cinemas	2188 3rd Street
Century Cinemas	3687 Avenue K
Countryside Cinemas	22 Hillside Street
Danforth Cinemas	P. O. Box 22
Dockside Movies	P. O. Box 224
Eastown Movie House	P. O. Box 429
Hillman Cinemas	55 Kemble Avenue
LaVista Cinemas	111 Vista Road
Liberty Cinemas	P. O. Box 998
Mainstream Movies	P. O. Box 33
Marquee Movies	1011 South Alameda Street
Midtown Moviehouse	1033 Commercial Street
Mooretown Movies	P. O. Box 11
O'Shea Movies	59 Erie
Redwood Cinemas	P. O. Box 112F
Renaissance Cinemas	3599 Woodward Avenue
Sunfest Cinemas	
Victory Cinemas	12119 South 23rd
Waterfront Cinemas	P. O. Box 3255
Wellington 10	1203 Tenth Southwest
Westview Movies	1112 Broadway

In Addition

Primary Key Field

When a table is created, usually one field is defined as the *primary key*. A primary key is the field by which the table is automatically sorted whenever the table is opened. The primary key field must contain unique data for each record. When a new record is being added to the table, Access checks to ensure there is no existing record with the same data in the primary key. If there is, Access will display an error message indicating there are duplicate values and will not allow the record to be saved. The primary key field cannot be left blank when a new record is being added, since it is the field that is used to sort and check for duplicates.

In BRIEF

Add a Record in Datasheet View
1 Open table.
2 Click New Record button.
3 Type data in fields.

1.5 Adding Records in Form View

Forms are used to enter, edit, view, and print data in tables. Forms are created to provide a user-friendly interface between the user and the underlying table of data. Adding records in a form is easier than using a datasheet since all of the fields in the table are presented in a different layout which usually allows all fields to be visible in the current window. Other records in the table do not distract the user since only one record displays at a time.

PROJECT: Worldwide Enterprises has just signed two new distributors in New York. You will add the information to the US Distributors table using a form.

S T E P S

1. With the **WEDistributors1** database open, click the Forms button on the Objects bar.

2. Double-click *US Distributors*.

   The US Distributors form opens with the first record in the US Distributors table displayed in the form. A Record Navigation bar appears at the bottom of the form.

3. Click the New Record button on the Record Navigation bar.

   A blank form appears in Form view and the Record Navigation bar indicates you are editing record number 22. Notice the New Record and Next Record buttons on the Record Navigation bar are dimmed.

4. Type **Movie Emporium** and then press Tab or Enter.

5. Type **203 West Houston Street** and then press Tab or Enter.

   Records are added to a form using the same navigation methods as those learned in the previous topic on adding records to a datasheet.

6. Type the remaining fields as shown below.

   When you press Tab or Enter after the *E-Mail Address* field, a new form will appear in the window.

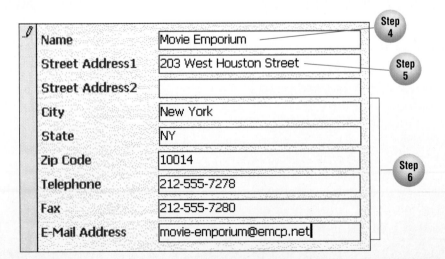

7 Type the following information in the new form for record 23:

Cinema Festival
318 East 11th Street
New York, NY 10003
212-555-9715
212-555-9717
cinemafestival@emcp.net

8 Click the First Record button  on the Record Navigation bar.

This displays the information for All Nite Cinemas in Form view.

9 Click the Last Record button ▶️ on the Record Navigation bar.

This displays the information for Cinema Festival in Form view.

10 Close the US Distributors form.

11 Reopen the US Distributors form.

12 Click the Last Record button on the Record Navigation bar.

Notice the last record displayed is the information for Westview Movies, not Cinema Festival. Access displays forms in the same manner as a datasheet—sorted by the primary key.

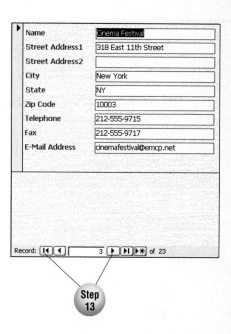

13 Click the First Record button on the Record Navigation bar, and then click the Next Record button two times to view the information for Cinema Festival.

Cinema Festival is record number 3 of 23 when it is sorted alphabetically on the *Name* field.

14 Scroll through the remaining records in Form view.

15 Close the US Distributors form.

Step 13

In Addition

Scrolling in Form View Using the Keyboard

Records can be scrolled in Form view using the following keyboard techniques:
- Page Down displays the next record
- Page Up displays the previous record
- Ctrl + End moves to the last field in the last record
- Ctrl + Home moves to the first field in the first record
- Type a record value in the Specific Record box on the Record Navigation bar

In BRIEF

Add a Record in Form View
1 Open form.
2 Click New Record button.
3 Type data in fields.

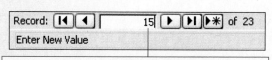

Type a record number here to move directly to a particular record if you know the record number value.

1.6 Deleting Records in Datasheet View

Records can be deleted in either Datasheet view or Form view. To delete a record, open the table in Datasheet view or Form view, activate any field in the record to be deleted, and then click the Delete Record button on the Table Datasheet toolbar or the Form View toolbar. Access will display a message indicating the selected record will be permanently removed from the table. Click Yes to confirm the record deletion.

PROJECT: The Countryside Cinemas and Victory Cinemas distributor agreements have lapsed and you have just been informed that they have signed agreements with another movie distributing company. You will delete their records in the US Distributors table.

STEPS

1. With the **WEDistributors1** database open, click Tables on the Objects bar.

2. Double-click *US Distributors*.

3. Click the insertion point in any field in the row for Countryside Cinemas.

    This selects record 4 as the active record.

4. Click the Delete Record button  on the Table Datasheet toolbar.

	Name	Street Address1	Street Address2	City	
	All Nite Cinemas	2188 3rd Street		Louisville	KY
	Century Cinemas	3687 Avenue K		Arlington	TX
	Cinema Festival	318 East 11th Street		New York	NY
▶	Countryside Cinemas	22 Hillside Street		Bennington	VT

5. Access will display a message box indicating you are about to delete 1 record and that the undo operation is not available after this action. Click Yes to confirm the deletion.

PROBLEM? Check that you are deleting the correct record before clicking Yes. Click No if you selected the wrong record by mistake.

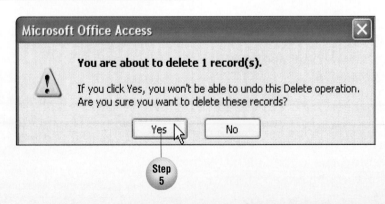

Microsoft Office Access

You are about to delete 1 record(s).

If you click Yes, you won't be able to undo this Delete operation. Are you sure you want to delete these records?

[Yes]   [No]

Step 5

6 Position the mouse pointer in the record selector bar for Victory Cinemas until the pointer changes to a black right-pointing arrow ➡ and then click the left mouse button.

> This selects the entire row.

7 Click Delete Record at the shortcut menu.

8 Click Yes to confirm the deletion.

9 Close the US Distributors table.

10 Click Forms on the Objects bar and then double-click *US Distributors*.

11 With the insertion point positioned in the *Name* field in the first record, click the Find button on the Form View toolbar.

12 Type **LaVista Cinemas** in the *Find What* text box and then click Find Next.

> The active record moves to record 8.

13 Close the Find and Replace dialog box.

14 Click the Delete Record button on the Form View toolbar.

15 Click No when prompted to confirm the deletion.

> The LaVista Cinemas record is restored in the table.

16 Close the US Distributors form.

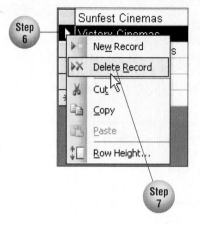

Step 6

Step 7

In Addition

More about Deleting Records

In a multiuser environment, deleting records is a procedure that should be performed only by authorized personnel; once the record is deleted, crucial data can be lost. It is a good idea to back up the database file before deleting records. Topic 1.11 on page 24 describes how to back up a database.

In BRIEF

Delete a Record
1 Open table in Datasheet view or Form view.
2 Click in any field in the record to be deleted.
3 Click Delete Record button.
4 Click Yes.

1.7 Sorting Records

Records in a table are displayed alphabetically in ascending order by the primary key field. To rearrange the order of the records, click in any field in the column you want to sort by and then click the Sort Ascending or Sort Descending buttons on the Table Datasheet toolbar. To sort on more than one column, select the columns first and then click the Sort Ascending or Sort Descending button. Access will sort first by the leftmost column in the selection, then by the next column, and so on. Columns can be moved in the datasheet if necessary to facilitate a multiple-column sort. Access will save the sort order when the table is closed.

PROJECT: You will perform one sort routine using a single field and then perform a multiple-column sort. To do the multiple-column sort you will have to move columns in the datasheet.

S T E P S

① With the **WEDistributors1** database open, click Tables on the Objects bar and then double-click *US Distributors*.

② Click in any row in the *City* column.

③ Click the Sort Ascending button on the Table Datasheet toolbar.

> The records are rearranged to display the cities starting with *A* through *Z*.

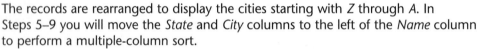

④ Click the Sort Descending button on the Table Datasheet toolbar.

> The records are rearranged to display the cities starting with *Z* through *A*. In Steps 5–9 you will move the *State* and *City* columns to the left of the *Name* column to perform a multiple-column sort.

⑤ Position the mouse pointer in the *State* column heading until the pointer changes to a downward-pointing black arrow and then click the left mouse button.

> The *State* column is now selected and can be moved by dragging the heading to another position in the datasheet.

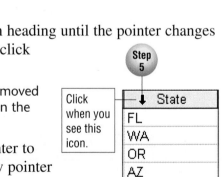

⑥ With the *State* column selected, move the pointer to the column heading *State* until the white arrow pointer appears.

⑦ Hold down the left mouse button, drag to the left of the *Name* column, and then release the mouse. *State* is now the first column in the datasheet.

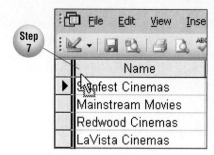

> A thick black line appears between columns as you drag, indicating the position to which the column will be moved when you release the mouse. In addition, the mouse pointer displays with a gray box attached to it, indicating you are performing a move operation.

⑧ Click in any field in the table to deselect the *State* column.

⑨ Move the *City* column between *State* and *Name* by completing steps similar to those in Steps 5–8.

⑩ Position the mouse pointer in the *State* column heading until the pointer changes to a down-pointing black arrow, hold down the left mouse button, drag right until the *State, City,* and *Name* columns are selected, and then release the left mouse button.

⑪ Click the Sort Ascending button.

> The records are sorted first by *State*, then by *City* within each state, and then by *Name* within each city.

⑫ Look at the four records for the state of New York. Notice the order of the records is Waterfront Cinemas in Buffalo first, then Cinema Festival, Movie Emporium, and Westview Movies in New York City next.

⑬ Close the US Distributors table. Click Yes when prompted to save the design changes.

In Addition

More about Sorting

When you are ready to conduct a sort in a table, consider the following:
• Records in which the selected field is empty are listed first.
• Numbers are sorted before letters.
• Numbers stored in fields that are not defined as numeric (i.e., social security number or telephone number) are sorted as characters (not numeric values). To sort them as if they were numbers, all field values must be the same length.

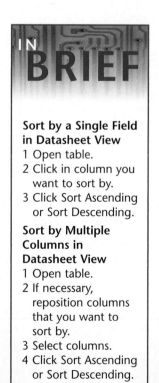

IN BRIEF

Sort by a Single Field in Datasheet View
1 Open table.
2 Click in column you want to sort by.
3 Click Sort Ascending or Sort Descending.

Sort by Multiple Columns in Datasheet View
1 Open table.
2 If necessary, reposition columns that you want to sort by.
3 Select columns.
4 Click Sort Ascending or Sort Descending.

1.8 Previewing and Printing; Changing Margins and Page Orientation

Click the Print button on the Table Datasheet toolbar to print the table in Datasheet view. To avoid wasting paper, use Print Preview to view how the datasheet will appear on the page before you print a table. By default, Access will print a datasheet on letter-size paper in portrait orientation with the top, bottom, left, and right margins at 1 inch. Change the margins and/or page orientation in the Page Setup dialog box.

PROJECT: Sam Vestering has requested a list of the US Distributors. You will open the table, preview the printout, change the page orientation, change the left and right margins, and then print the datasheet.

STEPS

1. With the **WEDistributors1** database open, open the US Distributors table.

   Notice the datasheet is displayed sorted by *State* first, then by *City*, and then by *Name* since the design changes were saved in the last topic.

2. Click the Print Preview button ⬚ on the Table Datasheet toolbar.

   The table is displayed in the Print Preview window as shown in Figure A1.3.

FIGURE A1.3 Print Preview Window

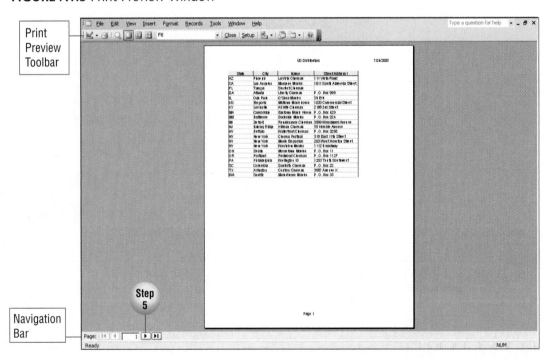

Print Preview Toolbar

Step 5

Navigation Bar

3. Move the mouse pointer (displays as a magnifying glass) 🔍 over the top center of the table and click the left mouse button.

   The zoom changes to 100% magnification. Notice that Access prints the table name at the top center and the current date at the top right of the page. At the bottom center, Access prints the word *Page* followed by the current page number.

4. Click the left mouse button again.

   The zoom changes back to *Fit*.

⑤ Click the Next Page button ▶ on the Navigation bar two times.

> The US Distributors table requires three pages to print with the default margins and the orientation. In Steps 6–8 you will change the orientation to landscape to see if all of the columns will fit on one page.

⑥ Click File and then Page Setup.

⑦ Click the Page tab in the Page Setup dialog box.

⑧ Click *Landscape* in the *Orientation* section and then click OK.

> Landscape orientation rotates the printout to print wider than it is taller. Changing to landscape allows more columns to fit on a page.

⑨ Look at the page number in the Navigation bar at the bottom of the Print Preview window. Notice that the page number is now 2. In landscape orientation, the US Distributors table will still need two pages to print.

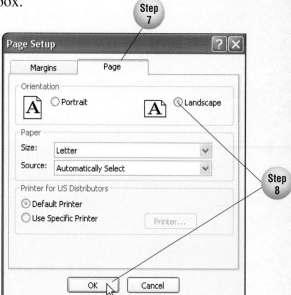

⑩ Click File and then Page Setup.

⑪ With the Margins tab in the Page Setup dialog box active, drag across *1* in the *Left* text box and then type **0.5**.

⑫ Press Tab, type **0.5** in the *Right* text box and then click OK.

> The Print Preview window still shows that the printout will require two pages.

⑬ Click the Print button 🖨 on the Print Preview toolbar.

> In a few seconds the table will print on the printer. Making the margins smaller than 0.5 inch would still not allow the entire datasheet to fit on one page. In Section 3 titled "Creating Queries, Forms, and Reports" you will learn how to create a report for a table. Use a report when you want control over which columns are printed and the data layout on the page.

⑭ Click Close on the Print Preview toolbar.

⑮ Close the US Distributors table.

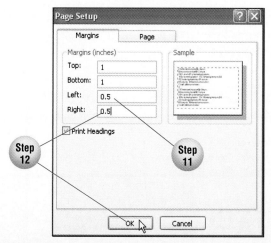

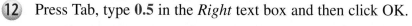

IN BRIEF

Change Margins
1 Click File, Page Setup.
2 Drag across 1 in *Top, Bottom, Left* or *Right* text box and type new value.
3 Click OK.

Change to Landscape Orientation
1 Click File, Page Setup.
2 Click Page tab.
3 Click *Landscape*.
4 Click OK.

1.9 Using Help

An extensive help resource is available whenever you are working in Access by clicking the text inside the *Ask a Question* text box located at the right side of the Menu bar, typing a term, phrase, or question, and then pressing Enter. This causes the Search Results task pane to open with a list of topics related to the text that you typed. Clicking a hyperlinked topic in the Search Results task pane opens a Microsoft Office Access Help window from which you can further explore information on the topic. By default, the search feature will look for information in all Office resources at Microsoft Office Online as long as you are connected to the Internet. In the *Search* list box at the bottom of the Search Results task pane you can change this setting to search only Offline Help resources.

PROJECT: After printing the US Distributors table, you decide it would look better if the height of the rows was increased to better space the records. You will use the Help feature to learn how to do this and then reprint the datasheet.

S T E P S

① With the **WEDistributors1** database open, open the US Distributors table.

② Click the text inside the *Ask a Question* text box (currently reads *Type a question for help*) at the right end of the Menu bar.

> When you click in the *Ask a Question* text box, an insertion point will appear and the text *Type a question for help* disappears. Once you have completed an initial search for help using the *Ask a Question* text box, the drop-down arrow will display a list of topics previously searched for in help.

③ Type **increase row height** and then press Enter.

> The Search Results task pane opens with a list of help topics related to the term, phrase, or question typed in the *Ask a Question* text box.

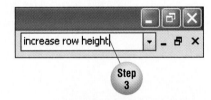

Step 3

④ Click the <u>Resize a column or row</u> hyperlink.

> As you move the mouse pointer over a help topic, the pointer changes to a hand with the index finger pointing upward. When you click a topic, the help information displays in a separate Microsoft Office Access Help window. You can continue clicking topics and reading the information in the Help window until you have found what you are looking for.

⑤ Click the <u>Resize rows</u> hyperlink in the Microsoft Office Access Help window.

> The Help window expands below the selected topic to display information on the feature including the steps to complete the task.

Step 4

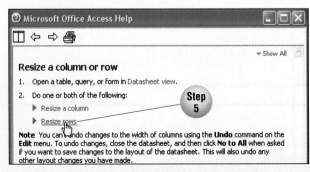

Step 5

⑥ Read the information below *Resize rows* in the Microsoft Office Access Help window.

If you would like a hard copy of the information, click the Print button on the Microsoft Office Access Help toolbar.

⑦ Click the Close button located on the Microsoft Office Access Help title bar.

⑧ Close the Search Results task pane.

⑨ Position the mouse pointer on the bottom row boundary for record 1 in the US Distributors table until the pointer changes to a horizontal line with an up- and down-pointing arrow attached (as shown in the Help window).

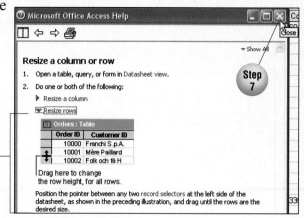

⑩ Drag the pointer down until the black line indicating the new row height is approximately at the position shown at the right and then release the mouse button.

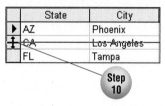

⑪ Click the Print Preview button to preview the datasheet.

⑫ Change the Page Setup to print the datasheet in *Landscape* orientation.

⑬ Print the US Distributors table.

⑭ Close the US Distributors table. Click Yes when prompted to save the layout changes.

In Addition

The Access Help Task Pane

Click Help on the Menu bar and then click Microsoft Office Access Help to open the Access Help task pane shown at the right. From this task pane you can access more extensive help resources such as online training courses for Access features, Microsoft Office newsgroups, download updates to your Office programs, and more.

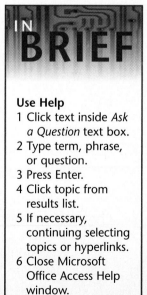

Use Help
1 Click text inside *Ask a Question* text box.
2 Type term, phrase, or question.
3 Press Enter.
4 Click topic from results list.
5 If necessary, continuing selecting topics or hyperlinks.
6 Close Microsoft Office Access Help window.

1.10 Compacting and Repairing a Database

Once you have been working with a database file for a period of time, the data can become fragmented because of records and objects that have been deleted. The disk space that the database uses may be larger than is necessary. Compacting the database defragments the file and reduces the required disk space. Compacting and repairing a database also ensures optimal performance while using the file. The database can be set to automatically compact each time the file is closed.

PROJECT: You will run the compact and repair utility on the WEDistributors1 database and then turn on the Compact on Close option so that the database is automatically compacted each time the file is closed.

STEPS

Step 2

1. With the **WEDistributors1** database open, click the Minimize button ▬ on the Microsoft Office Access 2003 title bar to reduce Access to a button on the Taskbar.

2. Right-click the Start button on the Taskbar and then click Explore at the shortcut menu. If the Start Menu window is not currently maximized, click the Maximize button on the Start menu title bar.

3. If necessary, scroll up or down the Folders pane and then click the drive and/or folder name where the **WEDistributors1.mdb** file is stored.

   If your data files are stored in a subfolder, click the plus sign to the left of the drive or folder name in the Folders pane to expand the display. Click the subfolder name to display the contents in the file list pane at the right.

4. Click View and then Details.

   This displays the file names with the file size, date, and time.

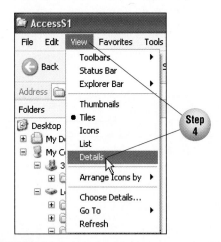

Step 4

5. Locate the file **WEDistributors1.mdb** and then write down the file size of the database.

   File size = _____

PROBLEM?

Two files will appear in the file list: **WEDistributors1.ldb** and **WEDistributors1.mdb**. The *.ldb* file is used to lock records so that two users cannot request the same record at the same time.

⑥ Click the button on the Taskbar representing Access.

⑦ Click Tools, point to Database Utilities, and then click Compact and Repair Database.

> A message displays on the Status bar indicating the progress of the compact and repair process. In a multiuser environment, no other user can have the database open while the compact and repair procedure is running.

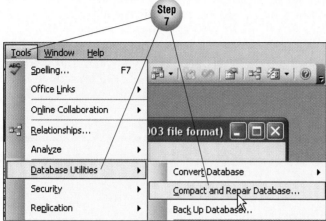

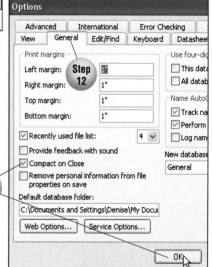

⑧ Click the button on the Taskbar representing the Explore window folder name or drive.

⑨ Write down the new file size of the **WEDistributors1.mdb** file. Notice that the amount of disk space is lower.

File size = _____

⑩ Click File and then Close to exit the Explore window.

⑪ With the **WEDistributors1** database open, click Tools and then Options.

⑫ Click the General tab in the Options dialog box.

⑬ Click the *Compact on Close* check box and then click OK.

> Turn on Compact on Close for each database so that the disk space the database uses is minimized.

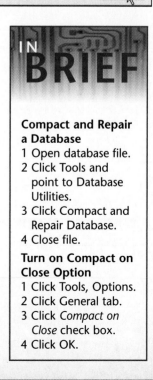

IN BRIEF

Compact and Repair a Database
1 Open database file.
2 Click Tools and point to Database Utilities.
3 Click Compact and Repair Database.
4 Close file.

Turn on Compact on Close Option
1 Click Tools, Options.
2 Click General tab.
3 Click *Compact on Close* check box.
4 Click OK.

1.11 Backing Up a Database

Regular backups of a database file should be maintained as part of the normal routine in a business setting for security and historical reasons. A loss of data as a result of theft, fire, breakdown in equipment, or other circumstance could have disastrous consequences. Damaged, lost, or stolen equipment can be replaced easily; however, it is the data stored on the computer that is the more valuable resource. Creating backups for historical reasons means that you have copies of a database before records are deleted, added, or edited. Access includes the Back Up Database command to facilitate the creation of a copy of the active database without having to leave Access. The Back Up Database feature automatically appends the current date to the end of the database file name to make the copy unique. The backup copy of the database is generally saved to an external media that can be stored away from the business operation for safekeeping.

PROJECT: You will create a backup copy of the WEDistributors1 database, using today's date for historical purposes, and then open the copy to check its content.

S T E P S

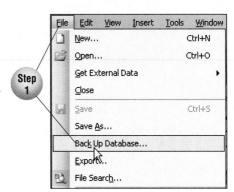

1. With the **WEDistributors1** database open, click File and then click Back Up Database.

   The Save Backup As dialog box opens. The default name in the File name *text box is the current database file name followed by an underscore character (_) and then the current date. Appending the current date to the file name means that you can create several historical copies of the database at key time intervals for reference. The* Save in *list box shows the current drive or folder name from which the active database was opened.*

2. Click the Save button in the Save Backup As dialog box with the default *Save in* and *File name* options.

   A message displays on the Status bar indicating the progress of the backup process. In a multiuser environment, no other user can have the database open while the backup procedure is running.

3. When the backup is complete, click File and then Close to close the **WEDistributors1** database.

   Notice the Compact process starts automatically when the file is closed since the Compact on Close feature was turned on in the last topic.

4. Click the Open button on the Database toolbar.

⑤ Click **WEDistributors1_
current date.mdb** in the file list
box where *current date* is
today's date—the date at which
the backup copy was made.

⑥ Click Open.

⑦ Open the US Distributors table.

> Notice the datasheet is the
> same as the US Distributors
> datasheet in **WEDistributors1**
> including the sort order and
> row height format.

⑧ Close the US Distributors table.

⑨ Click Tools and then Options.

⑩ If necessary, click the General tab
in the Options dialog box.

> Notice the *Compact on
> Close* check box is not
> selected.

⑪ Click the *Compact on Close*
check box and then click OK.

⑫ Close the **WEDistributors1_
current date.mdb** database.

⑬ Exit Access.

In Addition

Replicating a Database

A copy of a database can also be made by clicking Tools, pointing to Replication, and then clicking Create Replica. A *replica* is a copy of the database including all tables, queries, forms, reports, and so on. Replicas are generally created when you want to create a copy of a database for one or more remote users in cases where you cannot give access to the live data. For example, a sales representative who will be traveling with a laptop without network or dial-up access to the main database would need a replica. The database from which a replica is made is converted to a Design Master. Changes to the design of the database's objects can be made only in the Design Master. The difference between a replica of a database and a copy made with the Back Up Database command is that a replicated copy of a database can be synchronized with the Design Master. To continue with the previous example, the sales representative can enter orders from customers while on the road and then synchronize the replica copy with the Design Master when he or she returns to the office.

IN BRIEF

Back Up a Database
1 Open database file.
2 Click File, Back Up Database.
3 If necessary, change file name and location in Save Backup As dialog box.
4 Click Save.

FEATURES SUMMARY

Feature	Button	Menu	Keyboard
Add records	▶	Insert, New Record	Ctrl + +
Back Up Database		File, Back Up Database; or, Tools, Database Utilities, Back Up Database	
Column width		Format, Column Width	
Compact and repair		Tools, Database Utilities, Compact and Repair Database	
Delete records	✗	Edit, Delete Record	
Find	🔍	Edit, Find	Ctrl + F
Help	Type a question for help	Help, Microsoft Office Access Help	F1
Page Setup		File, Page Setup	
Print	🖨	File, Print	Ctrl + P
Print Preview	🔍	File, Print Preview	
Sort Ascending	A↓Z	Records, Sort, Sort Ascending	
Sort Descending	Z↓A	Records, Sort, Sort Descending	

PROCEDURES CHECK

Completion: The Access screen in Figure A1.4 contains numbers pointing to elements of the Datasheet window. Identify the element that corresponds with the number in the screen.

Horizontal scroll box   Office Assistant   Record Selector bar
Maximize   Close   Table Title bar
Field names   Active Record   New Record
Record Navigation bar   Scroll arrow   Minimize

1. _____   5. _____

2. _____   6. _____

3. _____   7. _____

4. _____   8. _____

FIGURE A1.4 Access Table

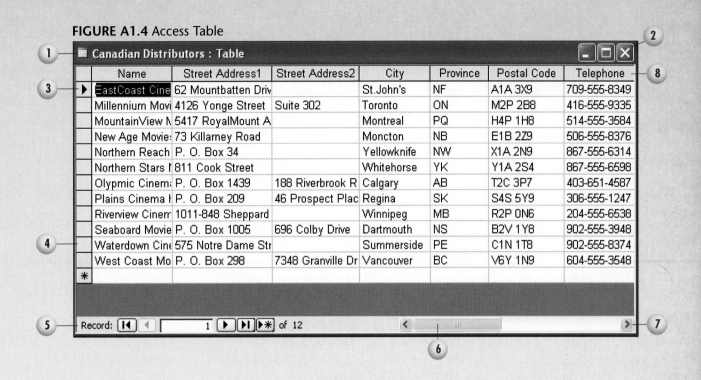

Identify the following buttons:

9. _____

10. _____

11. _____

12. _____

13. _____

14. _____

15. _____

SKILLS REVIEW

Activity 1: ADJUSTING COLUMN WIDTHS; FINDING AND EDITING RECORDS

1 Start Access and open the **WEEmployees1** database.
2 Open the Employee Dates and Salaries table.
3 Maximize the table.
4 Adjust all columns to Best Fit.
5 Find the record for Carl Zakowski and then change the birth date from *5/9/1967* to *12/12/1977*.
6 Find the record for Roman Deptulski and then change the salary from *$69,725.00* to *$71,320.00*. **(*Note: You do not need to type the dollar symbol, comma, and decimal.*)**
7 Find the record for Terry Yiu and then change the hire date from *4/12/2001* to *8/11/2001*.
8 Close the Employee Dates and Salaries table. Click Yes when prompted to save changes to the layout.

Activity 2: ADDING AND DELETING RECORDS

1 Open the Employee Dates and Salaries table.
2 Delete the record for Valerie Fistouris.
3 Delete the record for Edward Thurston.
4 Add the following employees to the table using Datasheet view:

1085	**1090**
Yousef J Armine	**Maria D Quinte**
11/19/1974	**4/16/1973**
3/14/2005	**11/29/2005**
European Distribution	**Overseas Distribution**
$42,796	**$42,796**

5 Close the table and then add the following record using the Employee Dates and Salaries form:

1095
Patrick J Kilarney
2/27/1981
12/12/2005
North American Distribution
$42,796

6 Close the Employee Dates and Salaries form.

Activity 3: SORTING; PREVIEWING; CHANGING PAGE ORIENTATION; PRINTING A DATASHEET

1 Open the Employee Dates and Salaries table.
2 Sort the table in ascending order by *Last Name*.
3 Sort the table in descending order by *Annual Salary*.
4 Sort the table in ascending order first by *Department* and then by *Last Name*.
5 Preview the table in the Print Preview window.
6 Change the orientation to landscape and then print the datasheet.
7 Close the Employee Dates and Salaries table without saving the changes to the design.

Activity 4: COMPACTING AND REPAIRING A DATABASE; BACKING UP A DATABASE

1 With the **WEEmployees1** database open, run the compact and repair database utility.
2 Turn on the Compact on Close feature in the Options dialog box.
3 Use the Back Up Database feature to create a copy of the database in the active drive and/or folder using today's date in the copied database file name.
4 Close the **WEEmployees1** database.
5 Open the backup copy of the **WEEmployees1** database created in Step 3.
6 Open the Employee Dates and Salaries table, view the table, and then close the datasheet.
7 Turn on the Compact on Close feature in the Options dialog box.
8 Close the backup copy of the **WEEmployees1** database.

PERFORMANCE PLUS

Assessment 1: ADJUSTING COLUMN WIDTH; FINDING AND EDITING RECORDS; USING PRINT PREVIEW

1 Jai Prasad, instructor in the Theatre Arts Division of Niagara Peninsula College, has been called out of town to attend a family matter. The grades for SPE266 have to be entered into the database by the end of today. Jai has provided you with the following grades:

Student Number	Final Grade
138-456-749	A+
111-785-156	C
378-159-746	B
348-876-486	D
274-658-986	B
349-874-658	C
255-158-498	C
221-689-478	A
314-745-856	B
325-841-469	A
321-487-659	F

2 Open the **NPCGrades1** database.
3 Open the SPE266 Grades table.
4 Adjust column widths so that all data is entirely visible.
5 Enter the grades provided in Step 1 in the related records.
6 Preview and then print the table.
7 Close the SPE266 Grades table. Click Yes when prompted to save changes.
8 Turn on the Compact on Close feature.
9 Close the **NPCGrades1** database.

Assessment 2: FINDING, ADDING, AND DELETING RECORDS

1 Dana Hirsch, manager of The Waterfront Bistro, has ordered three new inventory items and decided to discontinue three others. Dana has asked you to update the inventory database.
2 Open the **WBInventory1** database.
3 Open the Inventory List table.
4 Locate and then delete the inventory items *Pita Wraps; Tuna;* and *Lake Erie Perch.*
5 Add the following new records to the Inventory List table.

Item No	Item	Unit	Supplier Code
051	**Atlantic Scallops**	case	9
052	**Lake Trout**	case	9
053	**Panini Rolls**	flat	1

6 Adjust column widths so that all data is entirely visible.
7 Preview the table.
8 Adjust the top and bottom margin settings until all of the records will print on one page and then print the table.
9 Close the Inventory List table. Click Yes when prompted to save changes.
10 Turn on the Compact on Close feature.
11 Close the **WBInventory1** database.

Assessment 3: FINDING, SORTING, AND DELETING RECORDS; CHANGING ROW HEIGHT

1 You are the assistant to Bobbie Sinclair, business manager of Performance Threads. You have just been informed that several costumes in the rental inventory have been destroyed in a fire at a site location. These costumes will have to be written off since the insurance policy does not cover them when they are out on rental. After updating the costume inventory, you will print two reports.
2 Open the **PTCostumeInventory1** database.
3 Open the Costume Inventory table.
4 Locate and then delete the records for the following costumes that were destroyed in a fire at a Shakespearean festival:

Macbeth   Lady Macbeth   Hamlet   Othello   King Lear   Richard III

5 Sort the table in ascending order by *Character*.

6 Preview and then print the table.
7 Sort the table in ascending order first by *Date Out*, then by *Date In*, and then by *Character*.
8 Increase the height of the rows by approximately one-half their current height.
9 Save the changes to the design of the table.
10 Preview and then print the table.
11 Close the Costume Inventory table.
12 Turn on the Compact on Close feature.
13 Close the **PTCostumeInventory1** database.

Assessment 4: BACKING UP A DATABASE

1 You have been reading articles on disaster recovery planning in a computer-related periodical. Cal Rubine, chair of the Theatre Arts Division of Niagara Peninsula College, has advised you that the department does not currently have an up-to-date recovery plan for the information systems and has asked you to begin researching best practices. In the meantime you decide that the grades database needs to be backed up immediately.
2 Open the **NPCGrades1** database.
3 Create a backup copy of the database in the current drive and/or folder with today's date appended to the end of the file name.
4 Close the **NPCGrades1** database.
5 Open the backup copy of the **NPCGrades1** database.
6 Open and view each table to ensure the data was copied.
7 Turn on the Compact on Close feature.
8 Close the backup copy of the **NPCGrades1** database.

Assessment 5: FINDING INFORMATION ON DESIGNING A DATABASE

1 Use Access's Help feature to find information on the steps involved in designing a database.
2 The Help window for *About designing a database* lists several basic steps that should be followed when designing a database. Read the information presented in the first four links.
3 Use Microsoft Word to create a memo to your instructor as follows:
   • Use one of the memo templates.
   • Include an opening paragraph describing the body of the memo.
   • List the basic steps to designing a database in a bulleted list.
   • Briefly describe the first four steps.
4 Save the memo in Word and name it **AccessS1-P1Memo**.
5 Print and close **AccessS1-P1Memo** and then exit Word.

Assessment 6: CREATING A JOB SEARCH COMPANY DATABASE

1 You are starting to plan ahead for your job search after graduation. You have decided to start maintaining a database of company information in Access.

2 Search the Internet for company names, addresses, telephone numbers, and fax numbers for at least eight companies in your field of study. Include at least four companies that are out of state or out of province.

3 Open the **JobSearch1** database.

4 Open the Company Information table.

5 Enter at least eight records for the companies you researched on the Internet.

6 Adjust column widths as necessary.

7 Sort the records in ascending order by the *Company Name* field.

8 Preview the table. Change Page Setup options so that the entire table will fit on one page and then print the table.

9 Close the Company Information table.

10 Turn on the Compact on Close feature.

11 Close the **JobSearch1** database.

ACCESS SECTION 2

Creating Tables and Relationships

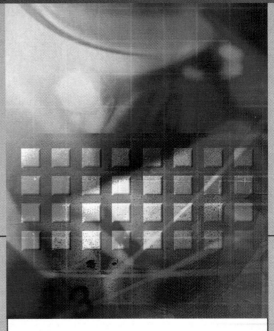

Tables in a database file are the basis upon which all other objects are built. A table can be created in three ways: using Design view, using the Table Wizard, or by entering data in a blank datasheet. When a common field exists in two or more tables, the tables can be joined to create a relationship. A relationship allows the user to extract data from multiple tables as if they were one. In this section you will learn the skills and complete the projects described here.

Note: Before beginning this section, delete any existing databases on your disk and copy each database as needed. Remember to remove the read-only attribute from each database after copying. If necessary, refer to page 1 for instructions on how to remove the read-only attribute. If necessary, check with your instructor before deleting any database files.

Skills

- Create a table in Design view
- Set the primary key for a table
- Limit the number of characters allowed in a field
- Enter a default value to display in a field
- Verify data entry using a Validation Rule property
- Restrict data entered into a field using an Input Mask property
- Set the Format property to control how data is displayed after it has been entered
- Confine data to a list of values using a *Lookup* field
- Enter data into a field by looking up data in another table
- Create a table using the Table Wizard
- Format a datasheet
- Create a one-to-many relationship between two tables
- Enforce referential integrity
- Create a one-to-one relationship between two tables
- Modify table structure by deleting fields
- Display records in a subdatasheet

Projects

Create and modify tables to store employee benefit information, employee addresses, employee review and training activities, and expenses; format a datasheet; create relationships between a Vendors and a Purchases table, an Employees and a Benefits table, an Employee and a Dates and Salaries table, and an Employees and an Expenses table; view records from a related table in a subdatasheet.

Create a table to store student grades for a course in the Theatre Arts Division.

Modify and correct field properties in the Costume Inventory table to improve the design.

Create a new database from scratch to track employee expense claims.

Create a Suppliers table in the Inventory database and create a relationship between the Suppliers table and the Inventory List table.

2.1 Creating a Table in Design View

Creating a new table in Design view involves the following steps: entering field names, assigning a data type to each field, entering field descriptions, modifying properties for the field, designating the primary key, and naming the table object. All of the preceding steps are part of a process referred to as "defining the table structure." Fields comprise the *structure* of a table. Once the structure has been created, records can be entered into the table in Datasheet view.

PROJECT: Rhonda Trask, human resources manager of Worldwide Enterprises, has asked you to review the employee benefit plan files and enter the information in a new table in the WEEmployees2 database.

STEPS

1. Open **WEEmployees2**.

2. With Tables already selected on the Objects bar, double-click *Create table in Design view*.

Tables is already selected on the Objects bar.

> This opens the Table1 : Table window, where the structure of the table is defined. Each row in the top section represents one field in the table.

3. With the insertion point already positioned in the *Field Name* column in the first row, type **Emp No** and then press Enter or Tab to move to the next column.

> The message at the right side of the *Field Properties* section changes at each column to provide information on the current option (see Figure A2.1).

PROBLEM

Do not type additional characters—field names can contain letters, numbers, and some symbols. Periods (.), commas (,), exclamation points (!), or square brackets ([]) are not accepted in a field name.

FIGURE A2.1 Field Properties Option Message

> The data type determines the kind of values that users can store in the field. Press F1 for help on data types.

Message changes at each column to provide help on the current item.

4. With *Text* already entered in the *Data Type* column, press Enter or Tab to move to the next column.

> Table A2.1 on page 37 provides a list and brief description of the available data types. The *Emp No* field will contain numbers; however, leave the data type defined as Text since no calculations will be performed with employee numbers.

⑤ Type **Enter the four-digit employee number** in the *Description* column and then press Enter to move to the second row.

> Entering information in the *Description* column is optional. The *Description* text appears in the Status bar when the user is adding records in Datasheet view.

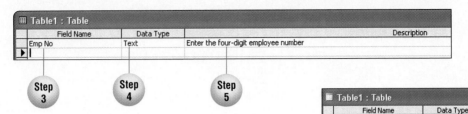

⑥ Type **Pension Plan** in the *Field Name* column in the second field row and then press Enter.

⑦ Click the down-pointing arrow at the right of the *Data Type* option box, click *Yes/No* in the drop-down list, and then press Enter.

> See Table A2.1 on page 37 for a description of the Yes/No data type.

⑧ Type **Click or press the spacebar for Yes; leave empty for No** and then press Enter.

⑨ Enter the remaining field names, data types, and descriptions as shown in Figure A2.2. Click the down-pointing arrow at the right of the *Data Type* option box to select data types other than Text.

FIGURE A2.2 Table Entries

Field Name	Data Type	Description
Emp No	Text	Enter the four-digit employee number
Pension Plan	Yes/No	Click or press the spacebar for Yes; leave empty for No
Dental Plan	Yes/No	Click or press the spacebar for Yes; leave empty for No
Premium Health	Yes/No	Click or press the spacebar for Yes; leave empty for No
Dependents	Number	Type the number of dependents related to this employee
Life Insurance	Currency	Type the amount of life insurance benefit for this employee

⑩ Click the insertion point in any character in the *Emp No* field row.

> This moves the field selector (right-pointing arrow) to the *Emp No* field. In Step 11, you will designate *Emp No* as the primary key field for the table.

⑪ Click the Primary Key button 🔑 on the Table Design toolbar.

> A key icon will appear in the field selector bar to the left of *Emp No*, indicating the field is the primary key for the table. The primary key is the field that will contain unique data for each record in the table. In addition, Access automatically sorts the table data by the primary key field when the table is opened.

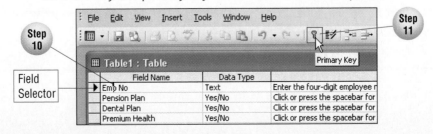

(continued)

(12) Click the Save button on the Table Design toolbar.

The Save As dialog box opens.

Table1 : Table

	Field Name	Data Type
🔑▶	Emp No	Text

Key icon indicates the field has been defined as the primary key.

(13) Type **Employee Benefits** in the *Table Name* text box and then press Enter or click OK.

Once the table is saved, the table name appears in the Title bar.

Save As   ? ✕

Table Name:
Employee Benefits| OK
                                      Cancel

Step 13

(14) Click the View button 🔲 on the Table Design toolbar.

The View button switches to Datasheet view, where you can enter records into the new table. The insertion point is automatically positioned in the first field for the first record. Notice the description *Enter the four-digit employee* number displays in the Status bar.

(15) Type **1001** and then press Enter.

(16) Press the spacebar or click the box in the *Pension Plan* column and then press Enter.

A check mark in the box indicates Yes, True, or On in a *Yes/No* field.

(17) Press Enter to leave the *Dental Plan* box empty and move to the next column.

An empty box indicates No, False, or Off in a *Yes/No* field.

(18) Press the spacebar or click the box in the *Premium Health* column and then press Enter.

(19) Type **2** in the *Dependents* column and then press Enter.

(20) Type **150000** in the *Life Insurance* column and then press Enter.

The dollar symbol, comma in the thousands, decimal point, and two zeros are automatically inserted in the field since the data type was defined as Currency.

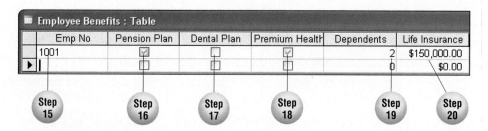

Employee Benefits : Table

	Emp No	Pension Plan	Dental Plan	Premium Health	Dependents	Life Insurance
	1001	☑	☐	☑	2	$150,000.00
▶		☐	☐	☐	0	$0.00

Step 15   Step 16   Step 17   Step 18   Step 19   Step 20

(21) Type the following two records in the datasheet:

Emp No	1005	*Emp No*	1010
Pension Plan	Yes	*Pension Plan*	Yes
Dental Plan	Yes	*Dental Plan*	No
Premium Health	Yes	*Premium Health*	No
Dependents	3	*Dependents*	0
Life Insurance	175000	*Life Insurance*	100000

(22) Close the Employee Benefits table.

Data Type	Description
Text	Alphanumeric data up to 255 characters in length, such as a name or address. Fields that will contain numbers that will not be used in calculations, such as a student number or telephone number, should be defined as Text.
Memo	Alphanumeric data up to 64,000 characters in length.
Number	Positive and/or negative values that can be used in mathematical operations. Do not use for values that will calculate monetary amounts (see Currency).
Date/Time	Stores dates and times. Use this format to ensure dates and times are sorted properly. Access displays an error message if an invalid date is entered in a Date/Time data field.
Currency	Values that involve money. Access will not round off during calculations.
AutoNumber	Access will automatically number each record sequentially (incrementing by 1) when you begin typing a new record. If you do not define a primary key and you respond Yes for Access to define one for you when you save the table, Access creates an AutoNumber field.
Yes/No	Data in the field will be either Yes or No, True or False, On or Off.
OLE Object	Used to embed or link objects created in other Office applications (such as Microsoft Word or Microsoft Excel) to an Access table.
Hyperlink	Field that will store a hyperlink such as a URL.
Lookup Wizard	Starts the Lookup Wizard, which creates a data type based on the values selected during the wizard steps. The Lookup Wizard can be used to enter data in the field from another existing table or display a list of values in a drop-down list for the user to choose from.

In Addition

Creating a Table by Adding Records

A new table can be created by typing directly into a blank datasheet. Double-click *Create table by entering data* in the Database window. Fields are initially named *Field1, Field2,* and so on. Access assigns data types and formats for each field based on the entry in each column when you save the datasheet. Rename a field by double-clicking the column header (e.g. *Field1*), typing a new name, and then pressing Enter. Open the table in Design view to edit the fields.

IN BRIEF

Create a Table in Design View
1 Open database or create a new database.
2 Click Tables on Objects bar.
3 Double-click *Create table in Design view*.
4 Type field names, descriptions, and assign data types in Table dialog box.
5 Assign primary key field.
6 Click Save button.
7 Type name for table and press Enter.

ACCESS

2.2 Modifying Field Size and Default Value Properties

Field properties are a set of characteristics used to control how the field displays or how the field interacts with data. For example, the *Field Size* property can be used to limit the number of characters that are allowed in a field entry. A field size of 6 for a customer number field would prevent customer numbers longer than 6 characters from being stored in a record. The *Default Value* property is useful if most records will contain the same value. The contents of the Default Value property appear in the field automatically when a

new record is added to the table. The user has the option of accepting the default value by pressing Enter or Tab at the field, or of overwriting the default by typing a different value.

PROJECT: Worldwide Enterprises uses a four-digit employee number. You will modify the *Emp No* Field Size property to set the maximum number of characters to *4*. Since most employees opt into the Pension Plan, you will set the default value for the *Pension Plan* field to *Yes*.

S T E P S

1. With **WEEmployees2** open, right-click the Employee Benefits table name in the WEEmployees2 : Database window and then click Design View at the shortcut menu.

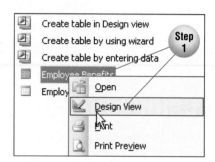

2. With *Emp No* already selected in the *Field Name* column, double-click the value *50* that appears in the *Field Size* property box in the *Field Properties* section and then type **4**.

   > Alternatively, click in the *Field Size* property box to activate the insertion point, delete 50, and then type 4.

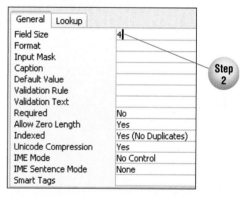

3. Click in the *Pension Plan* row in the *Field Name* column to display the Pension Plan properties in the *Field Properties* section.

   > Notice the list of available properties has changed. The items displayed in the *Field Properties* section in Table Design View change to reflect the options for the active field's data type. Since *Pension Plan* is a Yes/No field, the list of properties shown is different than those for *Emp No*, which is a Text field.

4. Click in the *Default Value* property box and then type **Yes**.

5. Click the Save button on the Table Design toolbar.

   > Since the field size for a field was changed *after* data has been entered into the table, Access displays a warning message that some data may be lost since the field size is now shorter.

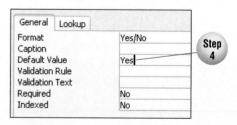

6 Click Yes to instruct Access to continue.

If a large amount of data was entered into a table before the field size was changed, make a backup of the file before changing the Field Size property. Check for errors by comparing the field data in the backup copy with the data in the working copy after Access saves the table.

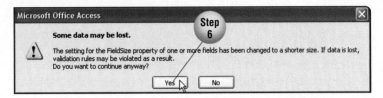

7 Click the View button 📊 to switch to Datasheet view.

Notice the *Pension Plan* column in the blank row at the bottom of the datasheet contains a check mark since the default value is now *Yes*.

8 Type **1020111** in the *Emp No* field in the blank row at the bottom of the datasheet and then press Enter.

A beep will sound each time you type a character that extends beyond the field size of 4 and Access does not display any characters in the field after the fourth character typed.

9 Press Enter to move to the *Pension Plan* field and then press Enter again to accept the default value of Yes.

Emp No	Pension Plan	Dental Plan	Premium Health	Dependents	Life Insurance
1001	☑	☐	☑	2	$150,000.00
1005	☑	☑	☑	3	$175,000.00
1010	☑	☐	☐	0	$100,000.00
1020	☑	☐	☐	0	$100,000.00

Employee Benefits : Table

Step 8   Step 9   Step 10

10 Enter the following data in the remaining fields:

Dental Plan	**No**	*Dependents*	**0**
Premium Health	**No**	*Life Insurance*	**100000**

11 Close the Employee Benefits table.

In Addition

Propagating Field Properties

The Property Update Options button appears whenever changes are made to an existing field. Click the button to automatically apply the same change to other objects within the database that are bound to the same field. Clicking the option to update the property everywhere the field is used displays a dialog box in which you can choose the objects that you want to inherit the change.

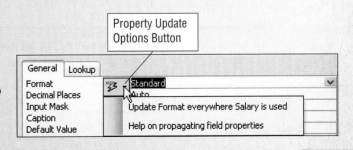

Property Update Options Button

General	Lookup
Format	Standard
Decimal Places	Auto
Input Mask	Update Format everywhere Salary is used
Caption	
Default Value	Help on propagating field properties

2.3 Validating Field Entries

The *Validation Rule* property can be used to enter a statement containing a conditional test that is checked each time data is entered into a field. When data is entered that fails to satisfy the conditional test, Access does not accept the entry and displays an error message. For example, suppose a customer number must be within a certain range of values. By entering a conditional statement in the validation rule property that checks each entry against the acceptable range, you can reduce errors and ensure that only valid numbers are stored in the customer number field. Enter in the *Validation Text* property the content of the error message that you want the user to see.

PROJECT: Worldwide Enterprises offers life insurance benefits up to a maximum of $199,999. You will add a validation rule and enter an error message in the validation text for the *Life Insurance* field in the Employee Benefits table to ensure no benefit exceeds this maximum.

STEPS

1. **WEEmployees2** open and the Employee Benefits table selected in the Database window, click the Design button on the Database window toolbar.

2. Click in the *Life Insurance* field row.

   The properties for the *Life Insurance* field display in the *Field Properties* section.

3. Click in the *Validation Rule* property box, type **<200000**, and then press Enter.

   Pressing Enter after typing the validation rule moves the insertion point to the *Validation Text* property box.

4. Type **Enter a value that is less that $200,000** and then press Enter.

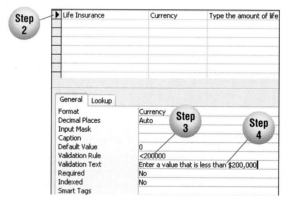

5. Click the Save button.

   Since a validation rule has been created *after* data has been entered into the table, Access displays a warning message that some data may not be valid.

6. Click Yes to instruct Access to test the data with the new rules.

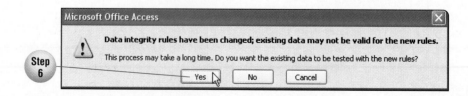

7 Click the View button to switch to Datasheet view.

8 Add the following record to the table:

Emp No	**1015**
Pension Plan	**Yes**
Dental Plan	**Yes**
Premium Health	**Yes**
Dependents	**2**
Life Insurance	**210000**

When you enter *210000* into the *Life Insurance field a*nd press Enter or Tab, Access displays an error message. The text in the error message is the text you entered in the *Validation Text* property box.

9 Click OK at the Microsoft Office Access error message.

10 Backspace to delete *210000*, type **199999**, and then press Enter.

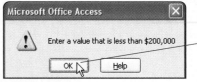

11 Close the Employee Benefits table.

Employee Benefits : Table

Emp No	Pension Plan	Dental Plan	Premium Health	Dependents	Life Insurance
1001	☑	☐	☑	2	$150,000.00
1005	☑	☑	☑	3	$175,000.00
1010	☑	☐	☐	0	$100,000.00
1020	☑	☐	☐	0	$100,000.00
1015	☑	☑	☑	2	$199,999.00

Step 8

Step 10

In Addition

Other Validation Rule Examples

Validation rules should be created whenever possible to avoid data entry errors. The examples below illustrate various ways to use the validation rule to verify data.

Field Name	Validation Rule	Data Check
Customer No	>1000 And <1100	Limits customer numbers to 1001 through 1099
Credit Limit	<=5000	Restricts credit limits to values of 5000 or less
State	"CA"	Only the state of California is accepted
Country	"CA" Or "US"	Only the United States or Canada is accepted
Order Qty	>=25	Quantity ordered must be a minimum of 25

IN BRIEF

Create a Validation Rule
1 Open the table in Design view.
2 Click in field row to select field.
3 Click in *Validation Rule* property box.
4 Type conditional statement.
5 Click in *Validation Text* property box.
6 Type error message.
7 Click Save.

2.4 Creating Input Masks; Formatting Fields

An *input mask* displays a pattern in the datasheet or form indicating how data is to be entered into the field. For example, an input mask in a telephone number field that displays (___)___-____ indicates to the user that the three-digit area code is to be entered in front of all telephone numbers. Input masks ensure that data is entered consistently in tables. In addition to specifying the position and amount of characters in a field you can create masks that restrict the data entered to digits, letters, or characters, and whether or not each digit, letter, or character is required or optional. Access provides the Input Mask Wizard to assist with creating the entry in the *Input Mask* property box.

The *Format* property controls how the data is *displayed* in the field *after* it has been entered.

PROJECT: You will create a new field in the Employee Benefits table for Pension Plan eligibility dates and include an input mask in the field indicating dates should be entered as *dd-mmm-yy*. To avoid confusion you will format the field to display the date in the same manner in which it was entered. Next, you will create an input mask for the *Emp No* field making all four characters required digits.

STEPS

1. With **WEEmployees2** open, open the Employee Benefits table in Design view.

2. Click in the *Field Name* column in the blank row below *Life Insurance*, type **Pension Eligibility**, and then press Enter.

3. Change the data type to *Date/Time* and then press Enter.

4. Type **Type date employee is eligible for pension plan in the format dd-mmm-yy (example: 12-Dec-05)**.

5. Click Save.

6. Click in the *Input Mask* property box in the *Field Properties* section and then click the Build button ⋯ .

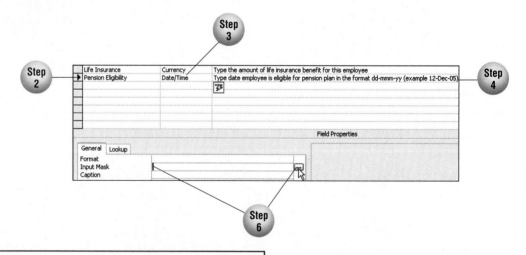

PROBLEM? Click Yes if a message displays informing you the feature is not installed and asking if you want to install it now. If necessary, check with your instructor.

7 Click *Medium Date* in the first Input Mask Wizard dialog box and then click Next.

> The input masks that display in the list in the first dialog box are dependent on the data type for the field for which you are creating an input mask.

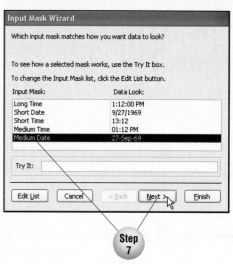

8 Click Next in the second Input Mask Wizard dialog box.

> This dialog box displays the input mask code in the *Input Mask* text box and sets the placeholder character that will display in the field. The default placeholder is the underscore character. Other available placeholder characters are #, @, and !. See In Addition on page 45 for an explanation of the symbols used in the *Input Mask* text box to create the medium date.

Step 7

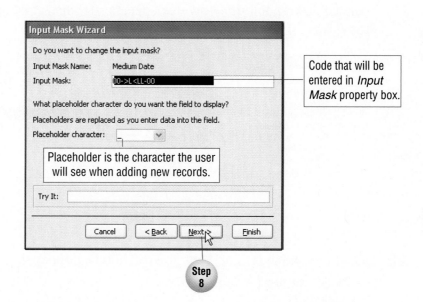

Code that will be entered in *Input Mask* property box.

Placeholder is the character the user will see when adding new records.

Step 8

9 Click Finish at the last Input Mask Wizard dialog box to complete the entry *00->L<LL-00;0;_* in the *Input Mask* property box.

10 Click the Save button and then click the View button to switch to Datasheet view.

11 Maximize the Employee Benefits table if it is not already maximized.

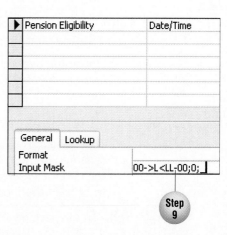

Step 9

(continued)

⑫ Click in the *Pension Eligibility* column for the first row in the datasheet.

The input mask __-___-__ appears in the field.

⑬ Type **22-jan-99** and then press the Down Arrow key.

The date *1/22/1999* displays in the field. By default, dates are displayed in the format *m/dd/yyyy*. To avoid confusion, in Steps 14–17 you will format the field to display the date in the same format that the input mask accepts the data.

⑭ Click the View button to switch to Design view.

The View button toggles between Datasheet view and Design view depending on which view is active.

⑮ With *Pension Eligibility* as the selected field, click in the *Format* property box, click the down-pointing arrow that appears, and then click *Medium Date* in the drop-down list.

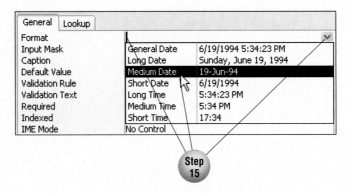

⑯ Click Save and then click View to switch to Datasheet view.

Notice the first Pension Eligibility date now displays as *22-Jan-99* instead of *1/22/1999*.

⑰ Click in the *Pension Eligibility* column in the second row in the datasheet and type **15feb99** and then press the Down Arrow key.

Notice the hyphens are not required to enter the date. In the next step you try to enter a date that does not conform to the input mask to test how Access restricts the entry.

⑱ Type **07/09/99** in the third row of the *Pension Eligibility* column.

A beep sounds as you type every character after *07*. The only characters Access has accepted in the field are *07* since the input mask requires that the next segment of the date be entered as letters in the format *mmm*. Notice the insertion point remains in the month section of the date.

⑲ Press Backspace twice to delete *07*, type **30jul99**, and then press Enter.

The difference between the input mask and the Format properties is that the input mask *restricts* the data that is entered into the field, while the Format property controls the *display* of the data after it is accepted into the field.

20 Best Fit the column width of the *Pension Eligibility* column.

In the next steps you will add an input mask to the *Emp No* field by typing input mask code directly into the field property box.

21 Click the View button to switch to Design view.

22 Click in the *Emp No* field row to display the related field properties.

To ensure that all employee numbers entered into the records are digits and not letters or symbols you will add the input mask using four zeros. Each zero represents a required digit. For example, an employee number of only two digits, such as *55*, would not be accepted. Refer to In Addition at the end of this topic for further explanation and examples of input mask code.

General	Lookup		
Field Size			4
Format	Step		
Input Mask	23		0000
Caption			

23 Click in the *Input Mask* property box and then type **0000**.

24 Click Save and then click View to switch to Datasheet view.

25 Click in the blank row at the bottom of the *Emp No* column and then type **abcd**.

A beep will sound as you type each letter since the input mask in the field requires that only digits zero through nine are allowed.

26 Press ESC twice to abort the new record and then close the Employee Benefits table.

In Addition

Input Mask Codes

The Input Mask Wizard is available only for fields with a data type set to Text or Date/Time. For fields such as Number or Currency you have to manually enter the mask. Following is a list of valid codes for an input mask and how each is used.

Use   To restrict data entry to
0   Digit, zero through nine, entry is required
9   Digit or space, entry is not required
L   Letter, A through Z, entry is required
?   Letter, A through Z, entry is not required
A   Letter or digit, entry is required
a   Letter or digit, entry is not required
&   Any character or space, entry is required
C   Any character or space, entry is not required
>   All characters following are converted to uppercase
<   All characters following are converted to lowercase

The mask created by the wizard in the *Pension Eligibility* field is broken down as *00-* (two required digits for the day) *>L<LL-* (three required letters for the month with the first letter uppercase and the remaining two letters lowercase) *00* (two required digits for the year). An input mask can have up to three sections separated by semicolons. In the second section *;0* zero instructs Access to store literal characters used in the field (hyphens between dates). The third section *;_* is the placeholder character.

IN BRIEF

Use Input Mask Wizard
1 Open table in Design view.
2 Enter field name, data type, and description.
3 Click Save.
4 Click in *Input Mask* property box.
5 Click Build button.
6 Click input mask you want to create.
7 Click Next.
8 Select placeholder character.
9 Click Next.
10 Click Next to store data without symbols.
11 Click Finish at last wizard dialog box.
12 Click Save.

2.5 Creating Lookup Fields

Create a *Lookup* field when you want to restrict the data entered into the field to a list of values from an existing table, or a list of values that you enter in the wizard dialog box. The Lookup tab in the *Field Properties* section in Table Design view contains the options used to create a *Lookup* field. Access includes the Lookup Wizard, which facilitates entering the option settings.

PROJECT: You will use the *Lookup* Wizard to create a new field in the Employee Benefits table that will display a drop-down list of vacation entitlements. Since the list will contain the only available vacation periods offered by Worldwide Enterprises you will further restrict the field by preventing items other than those in the list from being entered into the field.

STEPS

① With **WEEmployees2** open, open the Employee Benefits table in Design view.

② Click in the *Field Name* column in the blank row below *Pension Eligibility*, type **Vacation**, and then press Enter.

③ Click the down-pointing arrow at the right of the *Data Type* option box and then click *Lookup Wizard* from the drop-down list.

④ Click *I will type in the values that I want* and then click Next.

⑤ Click in the blank row below *Col1*, type **1 week**, and then press Tab.

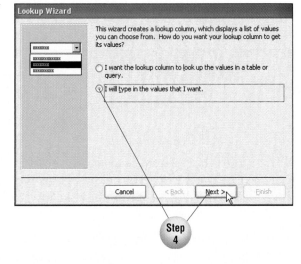

Step 4

PROBLEM ? If you press Enter by mistake and find yourself at the next step in the Lookup Wizard, click Back to return to the previous dialog box.

⑥ Type **2 weeks** and then press Tab.

⑦ Type **3 weeks** and then press Tab.

⑧ Type **4 weeks** and then click Next.

⑨ Click Finish in the last Lookup Wizard dialog box to accept the default label *Vacation*. No entry is required in the *Description* column.

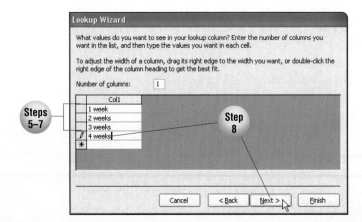

Steps 5–7

Step 8

10 Click the Lookup tab in the *Field Properties* section and view the entries made to each option by the Lookup Wizard.

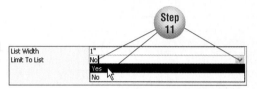

General	Lookup	
Display Control		Combo Box
Row Source Type		Value List
Row Source		"1 week";"2 weeks";"3 weeks";"4 weeks"
Bound Column		1
Column Count		1
Column Heads		No
Column Widths	Step 10	1"
List Rows		8
List Width		1"
Limit To List		No

Changes made to Lookup options through Lookup Wizard.

11 Click in the *Limit To List* property box, click the down-pointing arrow that appears, and then click *Yes*.

By changing the *Limit To List* property to *Yes* you are further restricting the field to only those items in the drop-down list. If a user attempts to type an entry other than 1 week, 2 weeks, 3 weeks, or 4 weeks, Access will display an error message and not store the data.

Step 11

List Width	1"
Limit To List	No
	Yes
	No

12 Click Save and then click View to switch to Datasheet view.

13 Click in the *Vacation* column in the first row in the datasheet, click the down-pointing arrow that appears, and then click *4 weeks* from the drop-down list.

Pension Eligibility	Vacation
22-Jan-99	
15-Feb-99	1 week
30-Jul-99	2 weeks
Step 13	3 weeks
	4 weeks

14 Press the Down Arrow key to move to the *Vacation* column in the second row, type **6 weeks**, and then press Enter.

15 Click OK at the message that displays informing you that the text entered is not an item in the list, and then click *3 weeks* from the drop-down list.

16 Display the datasheet in Print Preview. Change the page orientation to landscape and then print the datasheet.

17 Close the Print Preview window and then close the Employee Benefits table.

In Addition

Looking Up Data from Another Table

In this topic the items in the drop-down list were created by typing them in rows at the second Lookup Wizard dialog box. Items in the drop-down list can also be generated by specifying an existing field in another table or query. To do this, click Next at the first Lookup Wizard dialog box to accept the default setting *I want the lookup column to look up values in a table or query.* At the second Lookup Wizard dialog box, select the table or query name that contains the field you want to use. Specify the field to be used to generate the list in the third dialog box, and then set the column width at the preview of the list in the fourth dialog box. Creating field entries using this method ensures that data is consistent between tables and eliminates duplicate keying of information, which can lead to data errors.

In BRIEF

Create a List of Values Using Lookup Wizard
1 Open table in Design view.
2 Type field name and press Enter.
3 Click *Data Type* arrow.
4 Click *Lookup Wizard*.
5 Click *I will type in the values that I want* and click Next.
6 Type field values in *Col1* column and click Next.
7 Click Finish in last wizard dialog box.
8 Click Save.

2.6 Creating a Table Using the Table Wizard

Creating a table using the Table Wizard involves choosing the type of table from a list of sample tables and then selecting fields from the sample field list. Access creates the field names and assigns data types based on the samples. Once created, the fields in the table can be edited in Design view.

PROJECT: You will use the Table Wizard to create a new table that will store employee addresses.

S T E P S

1. With **WEEmployees2** open, double-click *Create table by using wizard*.

2. Click *Employees* in the *Sample Tables* list box.

3. Click *EmployeeNumber* in the *Sample Fields* list box and then click the Add Field button ⟩ to the right of the *Sample Fields* list box.

    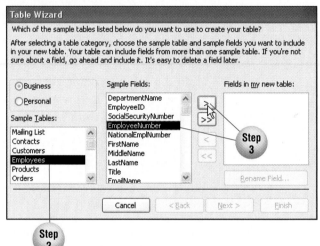

    This inserts the *EmployeeNumber* field in the *Fields in my new table* list box and moves the selected field in the *Sample Fields* list box to the next field after *EmployeeNumber*, which is *NationalEmplNumber*.

4. Double-click *FirstName* in the *Sample Fields* list box.

    Double-clicking a field name in the *Sample Fields* list box is another method of adding the field in the *Fields in my new table* list box.

5. Double-click the following field names in the *Sample Fields* list box.

    MiddleName
    LastName
    Address
    City
    StateOrProvince
    PostalCode

    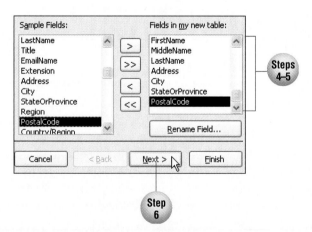

    PROBLEM Cannot locate some of the field names? You will need to scroll down the *Sample Fields* list box.

6. Click Next.

7. Click Next at the second Table Wizard dialog box to accept the table name *Employees* and *Yes, set a primary key for me*.

⑧ Click Next at the third Table Wizard dialog box to accept *not related to 'Employee Benefits'* in the *My new 'Employees' table is* list box since at this time we do not want to create a relationship between the new table and either of the two existing tables in the database.

⑨ Click *Modify the table design* at the fourth Table Wizard dialog box, and then click Finish.

> The new Employees table appears in the Design view window. When you elected to let Access set the primary key field, Access added the field *EmployeesID* to the table with the data type AutoNumber. An *AutoNumber* field automatically increments each field value by one each time a new record is added to the table. You decide this is a redundant field since each employee has a unique employee number. In Steps 10–13 you will delete the *EmployeesID* field and modify *EmployeeNumber* to make it the primary key field.

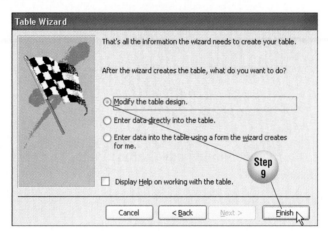

⑩ Click in the field selector bar next to *EmployeesID* and then click the Delete Rows button ⮕ on the Table Design toolbar.

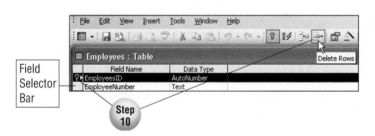

⑪ Click Yes to confirm the deletion.

⑫ Make the following changes to the *EmployeeNumber* field:

Field Name	**Emp No**
Field Size	**4**
Input Mask	**0000**

⑬ Make *Emp No* the primary key field.

⑭ Click the Save button.

⑮ Close the Employees table.

IN BRIEF

Create a Table Using Wizard
1 Open database file.
2 Double-click *Create table by using wizard*.
3 Click type of table in *Sample Tables* list box.
4 Add fields from *Sample Fields* list box to *Fields in my new table* list box.
5 Click Next.
6 Choose table name and primary key and click Next.
7 Choose to enter data directly in table or edit table in Design view.
8 Click Finish.

2.7 Formatting the Datasheet

The appearance of the datasheet can be changed using options on the Format menu. The default font and color of text in Access tables is 10-point Arial black. The Datasheet Formatting dialog box contains options to change the cell effect from the default flat appearance to raised or sunken appearance and alter the colors of the datasheet background and gridlines. Gridlines can be set to display horizontal lines only, vertical lines only, or both horizontal and vertical. The border and line styles of the datasheet, gridlines, and column headers can be changed from solid lines to a variety of other line styles.

PROJECT: You will change the appearance of the Employees datasheet by changing the background color, gridline color, font, and by freezing the first four columns so that scrolling right will not cause the *Employee Number, FirstName, MiddleName,* and *LastName* columns to disappear.

STEPS

① With the **WEEmployees2** database open, open the Employees table.

② Add the following information into a new record for *Emp No* 1001 in the table:

> **Sam Lawrence Vestering**
> **287-1501 Broadway**
> **New York, NY 10110**

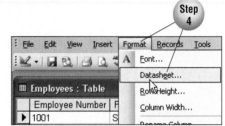

③ Adjust all of the column widths to Best Fit in the datasheet.

④ Click Format and then Datasheet.

⑤ Click the down-pointing arrow at the right side of the *Background Color* option box and then click *Aqua* in the drop-down list.

⑥ Click the down-pointing arrow at the right of the *Gridline Color* option box, scroll up the list box, and then click *Dark Blue*.

> The *Sample* section of the Datasheet Formatting dialog box displays the datasheet with the new settings.

⑦ Click OK to close the Datasheet Formatting dialog box.

⑧ Click Format and then Font.

⑨ Scroll down the *Font* list box and then click *Tahoma*.

⑩ Click *12* in the *Size* list box and then click OK.

> Notice some columns have to be readjusted after increasing the font size to redisplay entire field values.

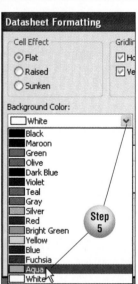

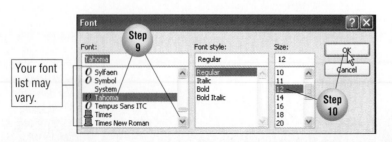

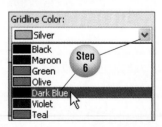

(11) Adjust all of the column widths to Best Fit.

(12) Position the mouse pointer in the *Employee Number* column heading until the pointer changes to a downward-pointing black arrow, hold down the left mouse button, drag right until the *Employee Number, First Name, Middle Name,* and *Last Name* columns are selected, and then release the left mouse button.

(13) Click Format and then Freeze Columns.

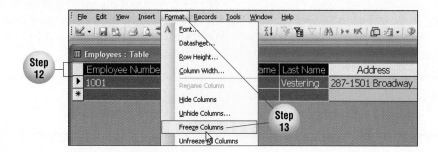

Step 12

Step 13

(14) Click in any field to deselect the first four columns.

(15) Select the *First Name, Middle Name,* and *Last Name* columns, click Format, click Column Width, type **20** in the *Column Width* text box, and then click OK.

(16) Change the column width of the *Address* column to *30*.

(17) Scroll right in the datasheet. Notice the first four columns remain fixed and do not disappear off the screen as you scroll.

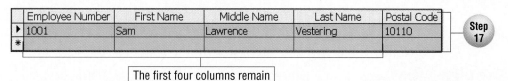

Step 17

The first four columns remain fixed as you scroll right.

(18) Display the datasheet in Print Preview and then change the page orientation to landscape. *(Note: Click Yes if you receive a message saying at least one column is too wide and data in the column will be cut off.)*

(19) Scroll the pages in Print Preview. Notice that the frozen columns, *Employee Number, First Name, Middle Name,* and *Last Name* repeat at the left edge of each page.

(20) Close the Print Preview window, click Format and Unfreeze All Columns, and then change all column widths in the datasheet to Best Fit.

(21) Display the datasheet in Print Preview. Change the left and right margins to 0.5 inch and then print the datasheet.

(22) Close the Print Preview window and then close the Employees table. Click Yes when prompted to save changes to the layout of the table.

(23) Close the **WEEmployees2** database.

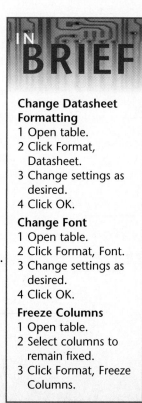

IN BRIEF

Change Datasheet Formatting
1 Open table.
2 Click Format, Datasheet.
3 Change settings as desired.
4 Click OK.

Change Font
1 Open table.
2 Click Format, Font.
3 Change settings as desired.
4 Click OK.

Freeze Columns
1 Open table.
2 Select columns to remain fixed.
3 Click Format, Freeze Columns.

2.8 Creating a One-to-Many Relationship

Access is sometimes referred to as a *relational database management system*. A relational database is one in which relationships exist between tables, allowing two or more tables to be treated as if they were one when generating reports or looking up data. Joining one table to another using a field common to both tables creates a relationship. Access allows for three types of relationships: one-to-many, one-to-one, and many-to-many. In a relationship, one table is called the *primary* table and the other table in called the

related table. In a one-to-many relationship, the common field value in the primary table is often the primary key field since only one record can exist for each unique entity. The related table can have more than one record for the corresponding field in the primary table.

PROJECT: You will create and print a one-to-many relationship between the Vendors table and the Purchases table in a database that is used to record purchase information.

STEPS

1. Open **WEPurchases2**.

2. Open the Vendors table, look at the field names and data in the datasheet, and then close Vendors.

3. Open the Purchases table, look at the field names and data in the datasheet, and then close Purchases.

    Notice that the Purchases table has more than one record for the same vendor number since buying goods and services from the same vendor several times within a year is possible. You will create a *one-to-many* relationship between the Vendors table and the Purchases table. Vendors is the primary table in this relationship since only one record for each vendor will exist. Purchases is the related table—many records for the same vendor can exist.

4. Click the Relationships button [icon] on the Database toolbar.

5. With *Purchases* already selected in the Show Table dialog box, click Add.

PROBLEM? Show Table dialog box does not appear? Right-click in Relationships window and then click Show Table at the shortcut menu.

6. Click *Vendors* and then click Add.

7. Click Close to close the Show Table dialog box.

    A common field in two tables is the basis upon which the tables are joined. In the next step, you will drag the common field *Vendor_No* from the primary table (Vendors) to the related table (Purchases).

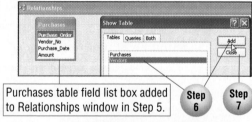

Purchases table field list box added to Relationships window in Step 5.

Step 6   Step 7

8. Position the mouse pointer over *Vendor_No* in the *Vendors* field list box, hold down the left mouse button, drag the pointer left to *Vendor_No* in the *Purchases* field list box, and then release the mouse button.

    The Edit Relationships dialog box appears when you release the mouse button.

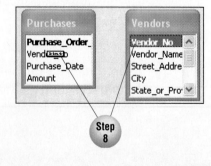

Step 8

⑨ Notice *One-To-Many* displays in the *Relationship Type* box of the Edit Relationships dialog box.

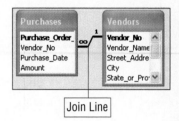

> Access determined the relationship type based on the common field that was used to join the tables. In the primary table (Vendors), *Vendor_No* is the primary key while in the related table (Purchases) *Vendor_No* is not the primary key. In the Purchases table, the field *Vendor_No* is referred to as the **foreign key**. A foreign key is the field used to relate a table and refers to the primary key in the other table.

⑩ Click the *Enforce Referential Integrity* check box in the Edit Relationships dialog box and then click Create.

> **Referential integrity** means that Access will ensure that a record with the same vendor number already exists in the primary table (Vendors) when a new record is being added to the related table (Purchases). If no matching record exists, Access will display an error message.

⑪ Click the Save button.

> A black line (referred to as a **join line**) joins the two tables in the Relationships window. A *1* appears next to the primary table, Vendors, indicating the *one* side of the relationship and the infinity symbol ∞ appears next to the related table, Purchases, indicating the *many* side of the relationship.

⑫ Click File and then click Print Relationships.

⑬ Click the Print button on the Print Preview toolbar.

⑭ Click the Close button on the Relationships for WEPurchases2 title bar. Click No when prompted to save changes to the design of the report.

⑮ Click the Close button on the Relationships window title bar.

⑯ Open the Purchases table.

> In Steps 17–19 you will test referential integrity by attempting to add a record for a vendor that does not exist in the primary table.

⑰ Click the New Record button, type **6552** in the *Purchase_Order_No* column, and then press Enter.

⑱ Type **150** in the *Vendor_No* column and then press Enter.

⑲ Press Enter through the *Purchase_Date* and *Amount* fields to move to the next row.

> Access displays an error message indicating you cannot add or change a record because a related record is required in the Vendors table.

⑳ Click OK to close the message window.

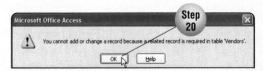

㉑ Close the Purchases table. Click OK at the error message that appears for the second time. Click Yes at the second error message box to close the object and confirm that the data changes will be lost.

㉒ Close **WEPurchases2**.

2.9 Creating a One-to-One Relationship; Deleting Fields

A one-to-one relationship exists when both the primary table and the related table will contain only one record for the common field. For example, in the WEEmployees2 database that has been used throughout this section, the Employees table would contain only one record for each employee. The Employee Benefits table and the Employee Dates and Salaries table would also contain only one record for each employee. If two of these tables are joined on the common *Emp No* field, a one-to-one relationship would be created.

PROJECT: You will create two one-to-one relationships in the WEEmployees2 database and then delete fields in the Employee Dates and Salaries table that are duplicated in the Employees table.

STEPS

1. Open **WEEmployees2**.

2. Click Tools on the Menu bar and then click Relationships.

3. With *Employee Benefits* already selected in the Show Table dialog box, hold down Shift and then click *Employees*.

4. Click the Add button in the Show Table dialog box.

5. Click the Close button in the Show Table dialog box.

   A field list box for each table is added to the Relationships window. In the next steps you will move and resize the field list boxes to make it easier to create the relationships.

6. Position the mouse pointer on the Title bar for the *Employees* field list box, hold down the left mouse button, and then drag the field list box down below the first two tables as shown.

7. Position the mouse pointer on the right border of the field list box for the *Employee Dates and Salaries* table (top right) until the pointer changes to a left- and right-pointing arrow, and then drag the border right until the Title bar shows the entire table name.

8. Move and resize the top two field list boxes as shown.

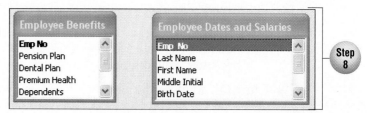

9. Position the mouse pointer over *Emp No* in the *Employees* field list box, hold down the left mouse button, drag the pointer to *Emp No* in the *Employee Dates and Salaries* field list box, and then release the mouse button.

10. Notice *One-To-One* displays in the *Relationship Type* box of the Edit Relationships dialog box.

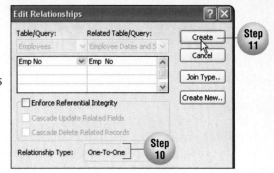
Step 11
Step 10

> Access determined the relationship type as one-to-one since the common field that was used to join the two tables is the primary key field in each table. In both tables, only one record can exist for each unique employee number.

11. Click Create.

> A black join line connecting the two *Emp No* fields appears between the two tables in the Relationships window. The join line does not show a *1* at each end similar to that shown in the previous topic because we have not turned on referential integrity. At this time we cannot turn on the referential integrity option since only one employee record exists in the Employees table while several employee records exist in the other two tables.

12. Position the mouse pointer over *Emp No* in the *Employees* field list box and then drag to *Emp No* in the *Employee Benefits* field list box.

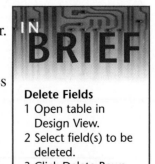
Step 14

13. Click Create in the Edit Relationships dialog box.

14. Move the field list boxes in the Relationships window as shown to spread out the join lines so that they are easier to see.

15. Print the Relationships. Refer to Steps 12–14 in the previous topic if you need assistance.

16. Click the Save button and then close the Relationships window.

17. Open the Employee Dates and Salaries table in Design view.

> Now that the Employee Dates and Salaries table is joined to the Employees table, you can delete the three fields relating to the employee names to avoid duplication of data. (In the next topic you will learn how to view data from two related tables in subdatasheets.)

18. Move the pointer in the field selector bar next to *Last Name* until the pointer changes to a right-pointing black arrow, drag down to *Middle Initial*, and then release the mouse.

19. Click the Delete Rows button on the Table Design toolbar.

20. Click Yes to confirm the deletion.

21. Click the Save button and then close the Employee Dates and Salaries table.

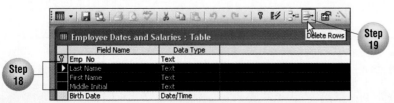
Step 18
Delete Rows
Step 19

IN BRIEF

Delete Fields
1 Open table in Design View.
2 Select field(s) to be deleted.
3 Click Delete Rows button on Table Design toolbar.
4 Click Yes to confirm deletion.

2.10 Displaying Records in a Subdatasheet

When two tables are joined, you can view the related records from the two tables within one datasheet window by displaying a *subdatasheet*. To do this, open one of the tables in Datasheet view. Click Insert on the Menu bar and then click Subdatasheet. Select the related table name in the Insert Subdatasheet dialog box and then click OK. A column appears between the record selector bar and the first field in each row displaying a plus symbol. Click the plus symbol (referred to as the *expand indicator*) next to the record for which you want to view the record in the related table. A subdatasheet opens below the selected record. To remove the subdatasheet, click the minus symbol (referred to as the *collapse indicator*) to collapse it (the plus symbol changes to a minus symbol after the record has been expanded).

PROJECT: You will open the Employees table in Datasheet view and then insert a subdatasheet to view the related benefits for Sam Vestering in the Employee Benefits table. While the subdatasheet is open you will update the benefit information to reflect the new life insurance for which Sam has subscribed, and then view the related dates and salary while in the same datasheet.

STEPS

① With **WEEmployees2** open, open the Employees table in Datasheet view.

② Click Insert and then click Subdatasheet.

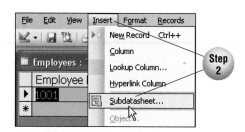

③ With the Tables tab selected in the Insert Subdatasheet dialog box, click *Employee Benefits* in the table list box and then click OK.

> A new column containing a plus symbol (+) appears between the record selector bar and the first field in the datasheet *(Emp No)*. The plus symbol is called the *expand indicator*. Clicking the expand indicator next to a record displays the related record in a subdatasheet from the table you chose in the Insert Subdatasheet dialog box.

④ Click the plus symbol (expand indicator) between the record selector bar and *1001* in the first row in the datasheet.

> The subdatasheet opens to display the record for the same employee (Emp No 1001) in the related table (Employee Benefits).

⑤ Drag across the value $150,000.00 in the *Life Insurance* field, and then type **190000**.

> One of the advantages to displaying subdatasheets is the ability to edit in a table while viewing related information from another table. Since the Employee Benefits table does not store fields with the employee names, viewing the benefit record in a subdatasheet from the Employees table which does display employee names ensures you are editing the correct record.

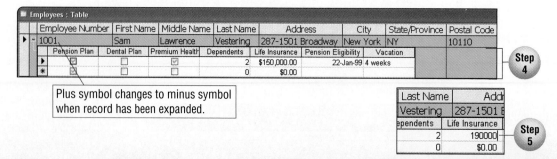

Plus symbol changes to minus symbol when record has been expanded.

6. Press Enter to complete life insurance entry.

7. With the Employee Benefits subdatasheet active, click Insert and then click Subdatasheet.

8. Click *Employee Dates and Salaries* in the table list box.

9. Click the down-pointing arrow at the right of the *Link Child Fields* option box and then click *Emp No* at the drop-down list.

10. Click the down-pointing arrow at the right of the *Link Master Fields* option box and then click *Emp No* at the drop-down list.

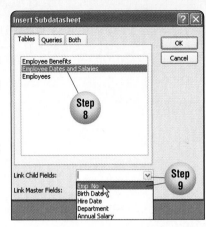

Since the common field *Emp No* did not appear automatically in the *Link Child Fields* and *Link Master Fields* list boxes, you need to instruct Access on the field to which the two tables should be linked. Access could not determine the linked field automatically since a relationship does not currently exist between Employee Benefits and Employee Dates and Salaries.

11. Click OK to close the Insert Subdatasheet dialog box. Click Yes at the message asking if you want Access to create a relationship for you.

A new column containing an expand indicator appears between the record selector bar and the first field in the subdatasheet *(Pension Plan)*.

12. Click the expand indicator between the record selector bar and the first row in the *Pension Plan* subdatasheet.

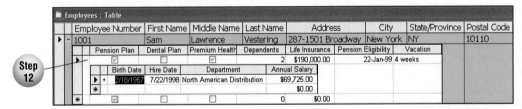

The subdatasheet opens to display the record for the same employee (Emp No 1001) in the related table (Employee Dates and Salaries). You are now viewing related information for one employee from all three tables in the database in one datasheet window.

13. Close the Employees table. Click Yes to save changes to all objects.

By saving the changes to all objects, expand indicators will now automatically appear in the datasheets alleviating the need to open the Insert Subdatasheet dialog box.

14. Open the Relationships window. Notice the new join line between the Employee Benefits and the Employee Dates and Salaries tables as a result of the subdatasheet you added in Step 11.

15. Close the Relationships window and then close **WEEmployees2**.

IN BRIEF

Display Records in Subdatasheet
1 Open table in Datasheet view.
2 Click Insert, Subdatasheet.
3 Click related table name.
4 Click OK.
5 Expand subdatasheet for desired record.
6 Edit and/or print as required.
7 Click minus symbol next to expanded record to collapse it.

FEATURES SUMMARY

Feature	Button	Menu	Keyboard
Datasheet view	▦	View, Datasheet View	
Delete rows	⇥	Edit, Delete Rows	
Design view	◣	View, Design View	
Font		Format Font	
Format datasheet		Format, Datasheet	
Freeze columns		Format, Freeze Columns	
Lookup Wizard		Insert, Lookup Field	
Primary key	🔑	Edit, Primary Key	
Relationships	⬚	Tools, Relationships	
Save table	💾	File, Save	Ctrl + S
Subdatasheet		Insert, Subdatasheet	
Table Wizard		Insert, Table, Table Wizard	

PROCEDURES CHECK

Completion: In the space provided at the right, indicate the correct term or command.

1. Display a table in this view to modify a field's properties. _____
2. Assign a field this data type if the field will contain dollar values that you do not want rounded off in calculations. _____
3. This is the term for the field in a table that must contain unique information for each record. _____
4. Enter a value in this field property if you want the value to appear automatically in the field whenever a new record is created. _____
5. Enter a conditional statement in this field property to prevent data that does not meet the criteria from being entered into the field. _____
6. An input mask that uses the character zero (0) means only this type of data is accepted into the field. _____
7. This is the name of the wizard used to create a drop-down list of entries that will appear when the user clicks in the field. _____
8. One table in a relationship is referred to as the primary table. The other table is referred to as this. _____
9. This type of relationship is created when the field used to join the two tables is the primary key in both tables. _____
10. The records in two related tables can be displayed in one datasheet window by clicking Insert and then this option. _____

11. Display this dialog box to change the appearance of the datasheet by modifying the background color and/or gridlines. _____

12. You can prevent columns from scrolling off the screen by selecting the columns you wish to remain fixed and then clicking this menu sequence. _____

SKILLS REVIEW

Activity 1: CREATING A TABLE IN DESIGN VIEW

1 Open the **WEEmployees2** database.
2 Create a table in Design view using the following field names and data types. You determine an appropriate description. Do not set any field properties since these will be changed in a later activity.

Field Name	Data Type	Field Name	Data Type
Emp No	Text	*Review Date*	Date/Time
Supervisor Last Name	Text	*Increment Date*	Date/Time
Supervisor First Name	Text	*Training Days*	Number

3 Define *Emp No* as the primary key field.
4 Save the table and name it *Review and Training*.
5 Switch to Datasheet view and then enter the following two records:

Emp No	1015	*Emp No*	1030
Supervisor Last Name	**Vestering**	*Supervisor Last Name*	**Deptulski**
Supervisor First Name	**Sam**	*Supervisor First Name*	**Roman**
Review Date	5/20/05	*Review Date*	1/24/05
Increment Date	7/01/05	*Increment Date*	3/03/05
Training Days	5	*Training Days*	10

6 Best Fit the column widths.
7 Close the Review and Training table. Click Yes when prompted to save layout changes.

Activity 2: CHANGING FIELD SIZE; VALIDATING ENTRIES; CREATING AN INPUT MASK; FORMATTING DATES

1 Open the Review and Training table in Design view.
2 Change the field size for the *Emp No* field to *4*.
3 Create a validation rule for the *Training Days* field to ensure that no number greater than 10 is entered into the field. Enter an appropriate validation text error message.
4 Save the table. Click Yes to test the data with the new rules.
5 Create the following input masks:
   a In *Emp No* create a mask that will ensure that four required digits only are entered into the field.
   b In *Review Date* and *Increment Date*, use the Input Mask Wizard to set the pattern for entering dates to *Medium Date*.
6 Change the format property for *Review Date* and *Increment Date* to display the date in the Medium Date format.
7 Save the table.

8 Switch to Datasheet view and add the following two records:

Emp No	1035	Emp No	1040
Supervisor Last Name	**Postma**	*Supervisor Last Name*	**Deptulski**
Supervisor First Name	**Hanh**	*Supervisor First Name*	**Roman**
Review Date	**14-Mar-05**	*Review Date*	**10-Mar-05**
Increment Date	**01-May-05**	*Increment Date*	**01-May-05**
Training Days	**8**	*Training Days*	**6**

9 Preview and then print the Review and Training table.
10 Close the Review and Training table.

Activity 3: CREATING A TABLE USING THE TABLE WIZARD; MODIFYING FIELD PROPERTIES; FORMATTING THE DATASHEET

1 Double-click *Create table by using wizard.*
2 Scroll down the *Sample Tables* list box and then click *Expenses.*
3 Add the following fields from the *Sample Fields* list box to *the Fields in my new table* list box and then click Finish:

EmployeeID	*AmountSpent*
ExpenseType	*DateSubmitted*

4 Switch to Design view to edit the table structure.
5 Make the following changes to the *EmployeeID* field:
   a Change the field name to *Emp No* and the data data type to *Text.*
   b Set the maximum number of characters allowed in the field to *4.*
   c Set an input mask that will accept four required digits only in the field.
6 Save the Expenses table and then switch to Datasheet view.
7 Add the following record to the Expenses table:

Employee ID	1001	Amount Spent	1,543.10
Expense Type	**Sales**	*Date Submitted*	**03/14/04**

8 Format the datasheet as follows:
   a Change the background color to silver.
   b Change the gridline color to maroon.
9 Change the font for the datasheet to 12-point Times New Roman.
10 Adjust any column widths that might be necessary after changing the font.
11 Preview and then print the Expenses table.
12 Close the Expenses table. Click Yes to save layout changes.

Activity 4: CREATING A ONE-TO-MANY RELATIONSHIP; DISPLAYING SUBDATASHEETS

1 Open the Expenses table in Design view.
2 With the *Emp No* field selected, click the Primary Key button to remove *Emp No* as a primary key field. **(Note: You are removing the primary key in the Expenses table so that the relationship that will be created in the following steps will be a one-to-many relationship. If Emp No remained as a primary key, Access would create a one-to-one relationship.)**
3 Click Save and then close the Expenses table.
4 Click the Relationships button on the Database toolbar.
5 Click the Show Table button , or click Relationships, Show Table to open the Show Table dialog box.
6 Add the Expenses table to the Relationships window and then close the Show Table dialog box.
7 Move the *Expenses* field list box to the right of the *Employees* field list box.

8 Create a one-to-many relationship by dragging the *Emp No* field name in the *Employees* field list box to the *Emp No* field name in the *Expenses* field list box.

9 Click *Enforce Referential Integrity* and then click Create in the Edit Relationships dialog box.

10 Print the Relationships.

11 Close the Relationships window. Click Yes to save changes to the report design and then click OK in the Save As dialog box to accept the default report name of *Relationships for WEEmployees2*.

12 Close the Relationships window.

13 Open the Employees table in Datasheet view.

14 Click Insert, click Subdatasheet, and then select the Expenses table in the Insert Subdatasheet dialog box.

15 Expand the subdatasheet for Emp No 1001.

16 Add the following record to the Expenses table using the subdatasheet:
Expense Type **Shipping**
Amount Spent **55.27**
Date Submitted **04/22/04**

17 Close the Employees table. Click No when prompted to save the layout changes.

18 Close the **WEEmployees2** database.

PERFORMANCE PLUS

Assessment 1: CREATING A TABLE IN DESIGN VIEW; CREATING A LOOKUP FIELD

1 Gina Simmons, instructor in the Theatre Arts Division of Niagara Peninsula College, has asked you to create a new table to store the grades for the MKP245 course she teaches. Gina would like to be able to select the student grade from a drop-down list rather than type it in.

2 Open the **NPCGrades2** database.

3 Create a new table in Design view using the following field names: *Student No*; *Last Name*; *First Name*; *Grade*. You determine the appropriate data type and descriptions for each field with the exception of the *Grade* field.

4 Use the Lookup Wizard in the *Grade* field to create a drop-down list with the following grades: A+, A, B, C, D, F. Set the *Limit To List* property for the *Lookup* field to Yes.

5 Define the *Student No* field as the primary key.

6 Save the table and name it *MKP245*.

7 Enter the following four records in Datasheet view:

Student No	111-785-156	*Student No*	118-487-578
Last Name	**Bastow**	*Last Name*	**Andre**
First Name	**Maren**	*First Name*	**Ian**
Grade	**A+**	*Grade*	**C**
Student No	137-845-746	*Student No*	138-456-749
Last Name	**Knowlton**	*Last Name*	**Yiu**
First Name	**Sherri**	*First Name*	**Terry**
Grade	**B**	*Grade*	**D**

8 Best Fit the column widths.

9 Preview, print, and then close the MKP245 table.

10 Close the **NPCGrades2** database.

Assessment 2: CHANGING FIELD SIZE; VALIDATING ENTRIES; CREATING AN INPUT MASK; FORMATTING DATES

1 Bobbie Sinclair, business manager of Performance Threads, has asked you to look at the design of the Costume Inventory table and try to improve it with data restrictions and validation rules. While looking at the design, you discover an error was made in assigning the data type for the *Date In* field.

2 Open the **PTCostumeInventory2** database.

3 Open the Costume Inventory table in Design view.

4 Change the *Date In* field to a Date/Time data field.

5 Change the field size for the *Costume No* field to *5*.

6 Performance Threads has a minimum daily rental fee of $85.00. Create a validation rule and validation text property that will ensure no one enters a value less than $85.00 in the *Daily Rental Fee* field.

7 To ensure no one mixes the order of the month and day when entering the *Date Out* and *Date In* fields, create an input mask for these two fields to require that the date be entered in the Medium Date format.

8 Since Performance Threads is open seven days a week, format the *Date Out* and *Date In* fields to display the dates in the Long Date format. This will add the day of the week to the entry and spell the month in full.

9 Save the table and then switch to Datasheet view.

10 Best Fit the columns.

11 Preview the datasheet. Change the margins for the page as necessary so that the entire datasheet fits on one page.

12 Print and then close the Costume Inventory table.

13 Close the **PTCostumeInventory2** database.

Assessment 3: CREATING A TABLE USING THE TABLE WIZARD; ESTABLISHING RELATIONSHIPS

1 Dana Hirsch, manager of The Waterfront Bistro, has asked you to create a new table in the inventory database that will store the supplier information. Since the Table Wizard provides a sample Suppliers table, you decide the wizard would be the most expedient method to use.

2 Open **WBInventory2**.

3 Create a new table using the Table Wizard. Use the Suppliers sample table and add the following fields to the new table: *SupplierID*; *SupplierName*; *Address*; *City*; *StateOrProvince*; *PostalCode*; *PhoneNumber*; *FaxNumber*.

4 Choose the option to set the primary key yourself, select the *SupplierID* field as the primary key field, and set the type of data to *Numbers and/or letters I enter when I add new records*.

5 Accept all other default settings in the wizard dialog boxes.

6 Switch to Design view for the new table.

7 Change the field name for *SupplierID* to *Supplier Code*, change the field size to *50*, and delete the entry in the *Caption* property box.

8 Enter the following record in the new table:

Supplier Code	1	*State/Province*	NY
Supplier Name	**Danby's Bakery**	*Postal Code*	14280
Address	**3168 Rivermist Drive**	*Phone Number*	(716) 555-4987
City	**Buffalo**	*Fax Number*	(716) 555-5101

9 Best Fit the column widths.

10 Preview the datasheet, change the page orientation to landscape, print, and then close the Suppliers table. Save the layout changes.

11 Display the Relationships window.
12 Create a one-to-many relationship using the *Supplier Code* field with the Suppliers table as the primary table and the Inventory List table as the related table. Enforce referential integrity when you create the relationship.
13 Click the Save button.
14 Print the relationships and then close the Relationships window. Click No to save the changes to the design of the report.
15 Close the **WBInventory2** database.

Assessment 4: CREATING A NEW DATABASE

1 Alex Torres, manager of the Toronto office of First Choice Travel, has asked you to help the accounting staff by creating a database to track employee expense claims information. You will create the database from scratch.
2 At a blank Database window, click the New button  on the Database toolbar.
3 Click the Blank database hyperlink in the New File task pane.
4 Type **FCTExpenses** in the *File name* text box in the File New Database dialog box and then click the Create button.
5 Look at the sample expense form in Figure A2.3. On your own or with another student in the class, make a list of the fields that would be needed to store the information from this form in a table. For each field on your list determine the appropriate data type and field properties that could be used.
6 Create a new table named **Expense Claims** in Design view. Use the information from Step 5 to enter the field names, data types, descriptions, and field properties.
7 Set an appropriate primary key field for the table and then save the table.
8 Switch to Datasheet view and then enter the expense information shown in Figure A2.3 in a record in the table.
9 Preview, print, and then close the Expense Claims table.
10 Turn on the Compact on Close feature.
11 Close **FCTExpenses**.

FIGURE A2.3 Assessment 4

Assessment 5: FINDING INFORMATION ON DELETING RELATIONSHIPS

1 Use the Help feature to find information on how to delete a relationship.
2 Print the Help topic that you find.
3 Open the **WEEmployees2** database.
4 Display the Relationships window and then delete the one-to-many relationship between the Employees and the Expenses tables.
5 Click Yes to confirm that you want to delete the selected relationship and then save the relationships.

6 Print the relationships. Click Yes to save the changes to the report name and accept the default name provided.
7 Close the Relationships window.
8 Close the **WEEmployees2** database.

Assessment 6: FINDING INFORMATION ON REQUIRED ENTRIES

1 Use the Help feature to find information on requiring that data be entered into a field. For example, you want to specify that a field cannot be left blank. *(Hint: Type require data in a field in the* **Ask a Question** *text box.)*
2 Print the Help topic you find.
3 Open the **WEEmployees2** database.
4 Open the Employees table in Design view.
5 You want to make sure that all records in the table have an entry in the *PostalCode* field, since you will be using this table to print mailing labels. Using the information you learned in help, change the field property for the *PostalCode* field to ensure that the field will have data entered in it.
6 Save the table and switch to Datasheet view.
7 Add a new record to the table using Emp No 9999. Use your name and address as the *Employee* information. When you reach the *PostalCode* field, try to press Enter to move past the field without entering any data. When Access displays the error message, click OK. Enter your postal code in the *PostalCode* field.
8 Change the page setup to fit all fields on one page and then print the Employees table.
9 Close the Employees table and then close the **WEEmployees2** database.

Assessment 7: CAR SHOPPING ON THE INTERNET

1 After graduation, you plan to reward yourself by buying a new car. Identify at least three different makes and models of cars that you like.
2 Search the Internet for the manufacturer's suggested retail price (MSRP) for the cars you would like to own, including whatever options you would order with the vehicle. *(Hint: Try searching by the manufacturers' names to locate their Web sites.)*
3 Create a new database in Access to store the information you find.
   • Click the New button on the Database toolbar, and then click the <u>Blank database</u> hyperlink in the New File task pane.
   • Type **NewCars** in the *File name* text box in the File New Database dialog box and then click Create.
4 Create a table named *New Car Pricing* using Design view. Include the manufacturer's name, brand, model of the car, options, and MSRP. Include other fields that you might want to track, such as color choice.
5 Best Fit the column widths.
6 Preview and then print the New Car Pricing table.
7 Close the New Car Pricing table and then close the **NewCars** database.

ACCESS

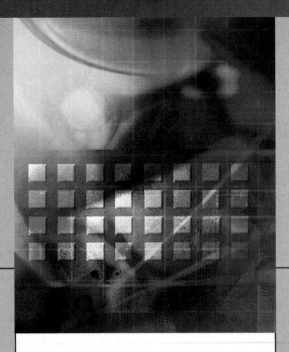

Creating Queries, Forms, and Reports

The ability to extract specific information from a table that can contain hundreds or thousands of records is an important feature in Access. Data is extracted from a table by performing a *query*. Creating a query is analogous to asking Access a question, such as *How many distributors are located in New York?* Forms are used to view, enter, and edit data. Generally, only one record at a time is displayed in a form. Forms can be designed to resemble existing forms used by the business, making the transition to an electronic database easier for employees. Reports are created to print the information in tables or queries in a variety of formats or styles. In this section you will learn the skills and complete the projects described here.

Note: Before beginning this section, delete any existing databases on your disk and copy each database as needed. Remember to remove the read-only attribute from each database after copying. If necessary, refer to page 1 for instructions on how to remove the read-only attribute. If necessary, check with your instructor before deleting any database files.

Skills

- Create, run, and print a select query in Design view
- Add multiple tables to a query
- Create and run a query using the Simple Query Wizard
- Sort the query results
- Add criteria statements to a query
- Delete fields from a query
- Perform calculations in a query
- Use aggregate functions in a query to calculate statistics
- Create an AutoForm
- Create a form using the Form Wizard
- Create a form with a subform
- Move and resize control objects in a form
- Modify properties of controls
- Add objects using the Control Toolbox
- Create and print a report using the Report Wizard
- Move and resize controls in a report

Projects

Create queries to extract fields from tables to print custom employee lists, add criteria, calculate pension contributions and monthly salaries, and perform statistical analysis on annual salaries and employee expenses; create and modify forms to facilitate data entry and viewing in the employees database; create and modify reports to produce custom printouts of employee and distributor data.

Create and print a query that will extract the records of students who achieved A+ in all of their courses.

Create a query, and create and print a report that lists all costumes rented in the month of August 2004; create and modify a form for browsing the costume inventory.

3.1 Creating a Query in Design View

A *query* is an Access object that is designed to extract specific data from a table. Queries can be created to serve a variety of purposes, from very simple field selection to complex conditional statements or calculations. When a table is viewed or printed in Datasheet view, all of the fields in the table are included. In its simplest form, a query selects only some of the fields from the table(s) to display or print. A criteria statement can be added to a query to display or print only certain records from the table(s). Queries can be saved for future use.

PROJECT: Rhonda Trask, human resources manager of Worldwide Enterprises, has asked for a list that includes employee number, employee name, date hired, department, and salary. This data is stored in two different tables. You will create a query to obtain the required fields from each table to generate the list.

STEPS

1. Open **WEEmployees3**.

2. Click the Queries button on the Objects bar.

3. Double-click *Create query in Design view*.

4. Double-click *Employees* in the Show Table dialog box with the Tables tab selected.

   A field list box for the Employees table is added to the top of the Query1 : Select Query window.

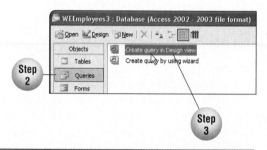

Step 2

Step 3

5. Double-click *Employee Dates and Salaries* in the Show Table dialog box.

   > Field list box for Employees table added in Step 4.

   A black join line with *1* at each end of the line between the Employees and the Employee Dates and Salaries tables appears illustrating the one-to-one relationship that has been defined between the two tables.

   Step 5   Step 6

6. Click Close to close the Show Table dialog box.

7. Double-click *Emp No* in the *Employees* field list box.

   Emp No is added to the *Field* row in the first column of the design grid. In Steps 8 and 9 you will practice two other methods of adding fields to the design grid.

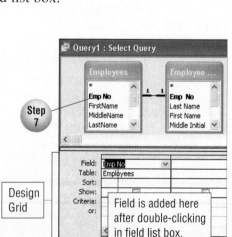

Step 7

Design Grid

Field is added here after double-clicking in field list box.

⑧ Position the mouse pointer on the *FirstName* field in the *Employees* field list box, hold down the left mouse button, drag the field to the *Field* row in the second column of the design grid, and then release the mouse button.

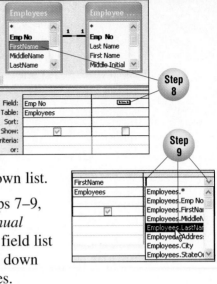

⑨ Click in the *Field* row in the third column of the design grid, click the down-pointing arrow that appears, and then click *Employees.LastName* in the drop-down list.

⑩ Using any of the three methods learned in Steps 7–9, add the fields *Hire Date*, *Department*, and *Annual Salary* from the *Employee Dates and Salaries* field list box to the design grid. You may need to scroll down the field list box to see the required field names.

⑪ Click the Save button on the Query Design toolbar.

⑫ Type **Trask Employee List** in the *Query Name* text box in the Save As dialog box and then press Enter or click OK.

⑬ Click the Run button [!] on the Query Design toolbar.

> The query results are displayed in Datasheet view as shown in Figure A3.1. The query results datasheet can be sorted, edited, or formatted in a manner similar to a datasheet. Data displayed in query results is not stored as a separate entity—the query is simply another interface for viewing and editing data in the associated table(s). When a saved query is opened, the query results are dynamically updated each time by automatically running the query.

⑭ Close the Trask Employee List : Select Query window.

FIGURE A3.1 Query Results Datasheet

Trask Employee List : Select Query

Emp No	First Name	Last Name	Hire Date	Department	Annual Salary
1001	Sam	Vestering	7/22/1998	North American Distribution	$69,725.00
1005	Roman	Deptulski	8/15/1998	Overseas Distribution	$69,725.00
1010	Hanh	Postma	1/30/1999	European Distribution	$69,725.00
1015	Lyle	Besterd	5/17/1999	North American Distribution	$44,651.00
1020	Angela	Doxtator	8/3/2000	North American Distribution	$45,558.00
1025	Jorge	Biliski	12/1/1999	North American Distribution	$44,892.00
1030	Thom	Hicks	1/22/1999	Overseas Distribution	$42,824.00
1035	Valerie	Fistouris	3/15/2001	European Distribution	$44,694.00
1040	Guy	Lafreniere	3/10/2001	Overseas Distribution	$45,395.00
1045	Terry	Yiu	4/12/2001	European Distribution	$42,238.00
1050	Carl	Zakowski	2/9/2002	European Distribution	$44,387.00
1055	Edward	Thurston	6/22/2002	Overseas Distribution	$42,248.00
1060	Donald	McKnight	6/22/2003	European Distribution	$42,126.00
1065	Norm	Liszniewski	2/6/2003	North American Distribution	$43,695.00
1070	Balfor	Jhawar	11/22/2004	Overseas Distribution	$44,771.00
1075	Mike	Fitchett	3/19/2004	Overseas Distribution	$42,857.00
1080	Leo	Couture	1/17/2004	European Distribution	$43,659.00
*					

Record: [◄] [◄] 1 [►] [►◄] [►*] of 17

IN BRIEF

Create a Query in Design View
1 Click Queries on Objects bar.
2 Double-click *Create query in Design view.*
3 Double-click required table(s) in Show Table dialog box.
4 Close Show Table dialog box.
5 Add required field names from field list box(es) to columns in design grid.
6 Click Save button.
7 Type query name and click OK.
8 Click Run button.

3.2 Using the Simple Query Wizard

Access includes the Simple Query Wizard to facilitate creating a query. At the first Simple Query Wizard dialog box, the table(s) and the fields within the table(s) are added to the query. Select a Detail or Summary query in the second dialog box. If you select Summary, click Summary Options to specify which field to group by and whether to calculate the sum, average, minimum, or maximum values in the group. Type the name for the query in the last dialog box.

PROJECT: Using the Simple Query Wizard, you will generate a list of each employee's name, number of dependents, life insurance, pension plan eligibility date, and vacation entitlement.

S T E P S

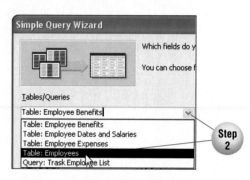

1. With **WEEmployees3** open and Queries selected on the Objects bar, double-click *Create query by using wizard*.

2. Click the down-pointing arrow at the right of the *Tables/Queries* text box and then click *Table: Employees* in the drop-down list.

3. With *Emp No* selected in the *Available Fields* list box, click the Add Field button ⟩ to move *Emp No* to the *Selected Fields* list box.

4. Click the Add Field button to move *FirstName* to the *Selected Fields* list box.

5. Click *LastName* in the *Available Fields* list box and then click the Add Field button.

6. Click the down-pointing arrow at the right of the *Tables/Queries* text box and then click *Table: Employee Benefits* in the drop-down list.

7. Double-click *Dependents* in the *Available Fields* list box.

   Double-clicking a field name is another way to move a field to the *Selected Fields* list box.

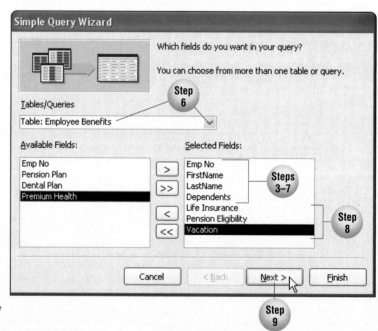

8. Move the following fields from the *Available Fields* list box to the *Selected Fields* list box:

   Life Insurance
   Pension Eligibility
   Vacation

9. Click Next.

10. Click Next at the second Simple Query Wizard dialog box to accept the default *Detail* report.

(11) Type **Employee Non-Medical Benefits** in the *What title do you want for your query?* text box, and then click Finish.

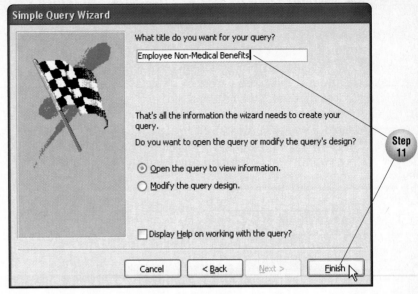

Simple Query Wizard

What title do you want for your query?

Employee Non-Medical Benefits

That's all the information the wizard needs to create your query.

Do you want to open the query or modify the query's design?

● Open the query to view information.

○ Modify the query design.

☐ Display Help on working with the query?

[Cancel]   [< Back]   [Next >]   [Finish]

Step 11

(12) View the query results in the datasheet and then click the View button on the Query Datasheet toolbar to switch to Design view.

In the next step you will modify the query design to sort the query results in ascending order by the employee's last name. In Query Design view notice that by using the wizard you added the tables and fields to the design grid through dialog boxes instead of using the techniques learned in the last topic.

(13) Click in the *Sort* row in the *LastName* column in the design grid, click the down-pointing arrow that appears, and then click *Ascending* in the drop-down list.

Step 13

Field:	Emp No	FirstName	LastName
Table:	Employees	Employees	Employees
Sort:			▾
Show:	☑	☑	Ascending
Criteria:			Descending
or:			(not sorted)

(14) Click the Save button on the Query Design toolbar and then click the Run button.

The query results datasheet appears with the records sorted by the *LastName* column.

(15) Close the Employee Non-Medical Benefits : Select Query window.

In Addition

Action Queries

In the last topic and in this topic, you have created *select* queries that displayed specific fields from a table. An *action* query makes changes to records in one procedure. There are four types of action queries: delete, update, append, and make-table. A delete query will delete a group of records from one or more tables. An update query is used to make global changes to a group of records in one or more tables. An append query adds a group of records from one or more tables to the end of one or more other tables. A make-table query will create a new table from all or part of the data in existing tables.

IN BRIEF

Create a Query Using the Simple Query Wizard

1 Double-click *Create query by using wizard.*
2 Choose table(s) and field(s) to include in query.
3 Click Next.
4 Choose *Detail* or *Summary* query.
5 Click Next.
6 Type title for query.
7 Click Finish.

ACCESS

3.3 Extracting Records Using Criteria Statements

All of the records in the tables were displayed in the query results datasheet in the two queries you have done so far. Adding a criterion statement to the query design grid will cause Access to display only those records that meet the criterion. For example, you could generate a list of employees who are entitled to four weeks of vacation. Extracting specific records from the tables is where the true power in creating queries is found since you are able to separate out only those records that serve your purpose.

PROJECT: Rhonda Trask has requested a list of employees who receive either three or four weeks of vacation. Since you already have the employee names and vacation fields in an existing query, you will modify the existing query to add the criteria statement and then save it under a new name.

S T E P S

1. With **WEEmployees3** open and Queries selected on the Objects bar, right-click the *Employee Non-Medical Benefits* query name, and then click Design View at the shortcut menu.

2. Maximize the query window if it is not already maximized.

3. Click in the *Criteria* row in the *Vacation* column in the design grid.

4. Type **4 weeks** and then press Enter.

   > The insertion point moves to the *Criteria* row in the next column and Access inserts quotation marks around *4 weeks* in the *Vacation* column. Since quotation marks are required in criteria statements for text fields, Access automatically inserts them if they are not typed into the *Criteria* text box.

5. Click in the *or* row in the *Vacation* column in the design grid (blank row below *4 weeks*), type **3 weeks**, and then press Enter.

   > Including a second criteria statement below the first one instructs Access to display records that meet either of the two criteria.

6. Click File and then Save As. Type **Employees with 3 or 4 weeks vacation** in the *Save Query 'Employee Non-Medical ...' To* text box in the Save As dialog box and then click OK.

7. Click the Run button on the Query Design toolbar.

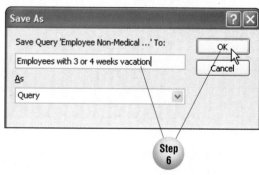

PROBLEM? Is the query results datasheet blank? Check the criteria statement in Design view. A typing error, such as *4 weks* instead of *4 weeks*, can cause a blank datasheet to appear.

8. View the query results in the datasheet and then click the View button on the Query Datasheet toolbar to switch to Design view.

   > Since Rhonda Trask is interested only in the employee names and vacation weeks, you will instruct Access not to display the other fields in the query results datasheet.

⑨ Click the check box in the *Show* row in the *Dependents* column to remove the check mark.

> Deselecting the check box instructs Access to hide the column in the query results datasheet.

Step 9

⑩ Deselect the *Show* check boxes in the *Life Insurance* and *Pension Eligibility* columns in the design grid.

⑪ Run the query.

⑫ Click the Print button on the Query Datasheet toolbar.

⑬ Close the Employees with 3 or 4 weeks vacation : Select Query window. Click Yes to save changes to the design of the query.

> Examples of other criteria statements are listed in Table A3.1.

TABLE A3.1 Criteria Examples

Criteria Statement	Records That Would Be Extracted
"Finance Department"	Those with *Finance Department* in the field
Not "Finance Department"	All *except* those with *Finance Department* in the field
"Fan*"	Those that begin *Fan* and end with any other characters in the field
>15000	Those with a value greater than 15,000 in the field
>=15000 And <=20000	Those with a value from 15,000 to 20,000 in the field
#05/01/05#	Those that contain the date May 1, 2005 in the field
>#05/01/05#	Those that contain dates after May 1, 2005 in the field

In Addition

Extracting Based on Two or More Criteria Statements

A query can be created that extracts records based on meeting two or more criteria statements at the same time. In the query design grid shown below, Access will display the records of employees who work in the North American Distribution department *and* who earn over $40,000. Typing two criteria in the same row means the record will have to satisfy *both* criteria to be displayed in the query results datasheet.

In BRIEF

Add a Criteria Statement to a Query
1 Open query in Design view.
2 Click in *Criteria* row in column to attach criteria to.
3 Type criteria statement.
4 Click Save button.
5 Click Run button.

Field:	FirstName	Address	Department	Annual Salary
Table:	Employees	Employees	Employee Dates and Salaries	Employee Dates an
Sort:				
Show:	☑	☑	☑	☑
Criteria:			"North American Distribution"	>40000
or:				

3.4 Performing Calculations in a Query; Deleting Fields

Calculations such as adding or multiplying two fields can be included in a query. To do this, in a blank field text box in Query Design view type the text that you want to appear as the column heading followed by a colon and then the mathematical expression for the calculated values. Field names in the mathematical expression are encased in square brackets. For example, the entry *Total Salary:[Base Salary]+[Commission]* would add the value in the field named *Base Salary* to the value in the field named *Commission*. The result would be placed in a new column in the query datasheet with the column heading *Total Salary*. The *Total Salary* column does not exist in the table used to create the query; the values are dynamically calculated each time the query is run.

In the last topic you deselected the *Show* text box to prevent a field from being displayed in the query results. If the field is no longer required it can be removed from the query design grid by selecting the field and then choosing the Cut command on the Edit menu.

PROJECT: Worldwide Enterprises contributes 8% of each employee's annual salary to a registered pension plan. You will modify the Trask Employee List query to include a calculation for the employer pension contribution.

STEPS

1. With **WEEmployees3** open and Queries selected on the Objects bar, open the Trask Employee List query in Design view.

2. Click File and then Save As.

3. Type **Employer Pension Contributions** and then click OK in the Save As dialog box.

   In the next step you will delete the *Hire Date* and *Department* columns in the design grid, since they are not required in the new query.

4. Position the mouse pointer in the gray field selector bar above the *Hire Date* field in the design grid until the pointer changes to a downward-pointing black arrow, hold down the left mouse button, drag right to select both the *Hire Date* and *Department* columns, and then release the mouse button.

5. Click Edit and then Cut.

   The selected columns are deleted from the design grid.

6. Click in the blank *Field* row next to the *Annual Salary* column in the design grid.

7. Type **Pension Contribution:[Annual Salary]*.08** and then press Enter.

PROBLEM**?** Message appears stating expression has invalid syntax? Check that you have used the correct type of brackets, typed a colon, and that there are no other typing errors.

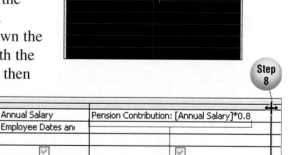

Step 3

Save As	? ✕
Save Query 'Trask Employee List' To:	OK
Employer Pension Contributions	Cancel
As	
Query	

Step 4

Hire Date	Department
Employee Dates ani	Employee Dates ani
☑	☑

Step 8

Annual Salary	Pension Contribution: [Annual Salary]*0.8
Employee Dates ani	
☑	☑

Step 7

8 Position the mouse pointer on the right vertical boundary line in the gray field selector bar above the *Pension Contribution* column until the pointer changes to a black vertical line with a left- and right-pointing arrow, and then double-click the left mouse button.

> Double-clicking the right field boundary line adjusts the width of the column to the length of the text in the field row.

9 Click the Save button and then click the Run button.

PROBLEM ?

> Does an Enter Parameter Value dialog box appear? A mistake in typing of *[Annual Salary]* in the calculated field will cause Access to display this dialog box, since it does not recognize the field name.

Properties

Step 12

Pension Contribution: [Annual Salary]*0.8

10 In the query results datasheet, click in any record in the *Pension Contribution* column, click Format, click Column Width, and then click Best Fit in the Column Width dialog box.

> The values in the calculated column need to be formatted to display a consistent number of decimal places. You will correct this in the next steps by changing the format option in the Pension Contribution's Field Properties sheet.

Step 13   Step 14

Field Properties

General | Lookup

| Description . . . . |
Format	
Decimal Places	General Number	3456.78
Input Mask	Currency	$3,456.
Caption	Euro	€3,456.
Smart Tags	Fixed	3456.79
	Standard	3,456.7
	Percent	123.00%
	Scientific	3.46E+0

11 Switch to Design view.

12 Click the insertion point anywhere within the *Pension Contribution* field row in the design grid and then click the Properties button on the Query Design toolbar.

13 Click in the *Format* property box, click the down-pointing arrow that appears, and then click *Currency* in the drop-down list.

14 Click the Close button on the Field Properties title bar.

15 Click the Save button and then click the Run button.

16 In the query results datasheet, click Format and then Font.

17 Click *12* in the *Size* list box and then click OK.

18 Adjust column widths as necessary so that all column headings are entirely visible.

19 Preview and then print the query results datasheet.

20 Close the Employer Pension Contributions query. Click Yes when prompted to save changes to the layout of the query.

IN BRIEF

Create a Calculated Field in a Query

1 Open query in Design view.
2 Click in first available blank *Field* row in design grid.
3 Type column heading for calculated field.
4 Type a colon (:).
5 Type mathematical expression.
6 Press Enter or click in another field.
7 Click Save button.
8 Click Run button.

3.5 Calculating Statistics Using Aggregate Functions

Aggregate functions such as Sum, Avg, Min, Max, or Count can be included in a query to calculate statistics from numeric field values of all of the records in the table. When an aggregate function is used, Access displays one row in the query results datasheet with the formula result for the function used. To display the aggregate function list, click the Totals button on the Query Design toolbar. Access adds a *Total* row to the design grid with a drop-down list from which you select the desired function.

Using the *Group By* option in the *Total* drop-down list you can add a field to the query upon which you want Access to group records for statistical calculations.

PROJECT: Rhonda Trask has asked for statistics on the salaries currently paid to employees. You will create a new query in Design view and use aggregate functions to find the total of all salaries, the average salary, and the maximum and minimum salaries. In a second query you will calculate the same statistics by department.

STEPS

1 With **WEEmployees3** open and Queries selected on the Objects bar, double-click *Create query in design view*.

2 At the Show Table dialog box with the Tables tab selected, click *Employee Dates and Salaries,* click the Add button, and then click the Close button.

> The field upon which the statistics are to be calculated is added to the design grid once for each aggregate function you want to use.

Field:	Annual Salary	Annual Salary	Annual Salary	Annual Salary	Step 3
Table:	Employee Dates an	Employee Dates an	Employee Dates an	Employee Dates an	
Sort:					
Show:	☑	☑	☑	☑	

3 Scroll down to the bottom of the *Employee Dates and Salaries* field list box and then double-click *Annual Salary* four times.

4 Click the Totals button **Σ** on the Query Design toolbar.

> A *Total* row is added to the design grid between *Table* and *Sort* with the default option *Group By.*

Field:	Annual Salary
Table:	Employee Dates an
Total:	Group By
Sort:	Group By
Show:	**Sum**
Criteria:	Avg
or:	Min
	Max Step 5
	Count
	StDev
	Var

5 Click in the *Total* row in the first *Annual Salary* column in the design grid, click the down-pointing arrow that appears, and then click *Sum* in the drop-down list.

6 Click in the *Total* row in the second *Annual Salary* column, click the down-pointing arrow that appears, and then click *Avg* in the drop-down list.

7 Change the *Total* option to *Max* for the third *Annual Salary* column.

8 Change the *Total* option to *Min* for the fourth *Annual Salary* column.

9 Click the Save button on the Query Design toolbar, type **Annual Salary Statistics** in the *Query Name* text box in the Save As dialog box, and then press Enter or click OK.

10 Click the Run button.

SumOfAnnual S	AvgOfAnnual Sa	MaxOfAnnual S	MinOfAnnual Sa	Step 10
$823,170.00	$48,421.76	$69,725.00	$42,126.00	

> Access calculates the Sum, Avg, Max, and Min functions for all annual salary values in the table and displays one row with the results. By default Access assigns column headings in the datasheet using the function name, the word *Of*, and the field name from which the function has been derived such as *SumOfAnnual Salary, AvgOfAnnual Salary, MaxOfAnnual Salary,* and *MinOfAnnual Salary.*

11. Switch to Design view.

12. Click in any row in the first column in the design grid and then click the Properties button on the Query Design toolbar.

13. Click in the *Caption* property box, type **Total Annual Salaries**, and then click the Close button on the Field Properties title bar.

Field Properties

General | Lookup

Description . . . .
Format . . . .
Decimal Places . . . .
Input Mask . . . .
Caption . . . . Total Annual Salaries
Smart Tags . . . .

Step 13

Close

14. Right-click over any row in the second column in the design grid, click Properties at the shortcut menu, click in the *Caption* property box, type **Average Annual Salary**, and then click the Close button on the Field Properties Title bar.

15. Repeat Step 14 to change the *Caption* field property for the third and fourth columns to **Maximum Annual Salary** and **Minimum Annual Salary**, respectively.

16. Click the Save button and then click the Run button.

17. In the query results datasheet, change the font size to *12*, Best Fit all column widths, change the page orientation to landscape, and then print the query results datasheet.

18. Switch to Design view.

Total Annual Salaries	Average Annual Salary	Maximum Annual Salary	Minimum Annual Salary
$823,170.00	$48,421.76	$69,725.00	$42,126.00

Steps 14–17

19. Double-click *Department* in the field list box for the Employee Dates and Salaries table.

> The *Department* field is added to the design grid with *Total* automatically set to *Group By*. Adding this field produces a row in the query results datasheet for each department in which Access calculates the total, average, maximum, and minimum salary.

20. Click File and then Save As. Click in the *Save Query 'Annual Salary Statistics' To* text box at the end of the current query name, press the spacebar once, type **by Department**, and then press Enter or click OK.

21. Click the Run button.

22. Best Fit the *Department* column in the query results datasheet, change the left and right margins to 0.5 inch, and then print the query results datasheet.

23. Close the Annual Salary Statistics by Department query. Click Yes when prompted to save changes to the layout of the query.

3.6 Creating Forms Using AutoForm and the Form Wizard

As you saw in Section 1, forms provide a more user-friendly interface than a datasheet for viewing, adding, editing, and deleting records since only one record is displayed at a time and generally all fields are visible in one screen. AutoForm creates a new form by automatically including all of the fields from the specified table. The layout and style are predefined based on the selection of AutoForm: Columnar; AutoForm: Tabular; AutoForm: Datasheet; AutoForm: PivotTable; or AutoForm: PivotChart in the New Form dialog box.

The Form Wizard provides more choices for the form design than AutoForm. In the Form Wizard

the user is guided through a series of dialog boxes to generate the form, including selecting the table and fields that will be used to make up the form; choosing a layout for the fields; selecting the form style from various colors and backgrounds; and entering a title for the form.

PROJECT: You will create an Autoform using the Employee Dates and Salaries table; another form for the Employee Benefits table using the Form Wizard; and a form with a subform for employees and expenses using the Form Wizard.

STEPS

① With **WEEmployees3** open, click Forms on the Objects bar.

② Click the New button on the Database window toolbar.

③ Click *AutoForm: Columnar* in the New Form dialog box list box.

④ Click the down-pointing arrow next to *Choose the table or query where the object's data comes from*, click *Employee Dates and Salaries* in the drop-down list, and then click OK.

> In a few seconds the Employee Dates and Salaries form appears, with the data from the first record in the table displayed in the form as shown in Figure A3.2.

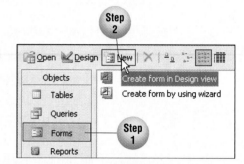

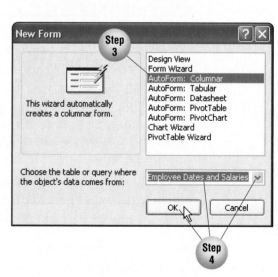

FIGURE A3.2 Employee Dates and Salaries Form

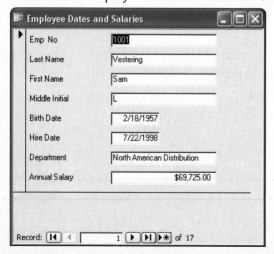

(5) Click the Next Record button ▶ on the Record Navigation bar a few times to scroll the records in the table. When you are finished scrolling records, click the Close button on the Employee Dates and Salaries form Title bar.

(6) Click Yes to save changes to the design of the form and then click OK in the Save As dialog box to accept the default form name *Employee Dates and Salaries*.

(7) At the WEEmployees3 database window, with Forms still selected on the Objects bar, double-click *Create form by using wizard*.

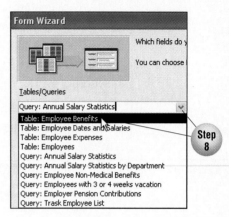

(8) Click the down-pointing arrow at the right of the *Tables/Queries* text box and then click *Table: Employee Benefits* in the drop-down list.

> The list of fields in the *Available Fields* list box changes to the field names for the Employee Benefits table. In the next step you will choose which fields to include in the form.

(9) Click the Add All Fields button >> to move all of the fields in the *Available Fields* list box to the *Selected Fields* list box and then click Next.

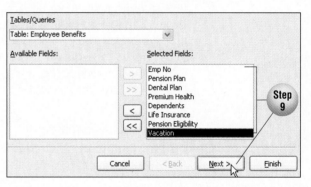

(10) Click *Tabular* in the second Form Wizard dialog box to view the tabular layout in the preview window.

(11) Click *Datasheet* to preview the datasheet layout.

(12) Click *Justified* to preview the justified layout.

(13) Click *Columnar* and then click Next.

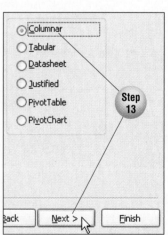

(14) Click each of the styles in the list box in the third Form Wizard dialog box to preview each style's colors and backgrounds in the preview window.

(15) Click *Industrial* and then click Next.

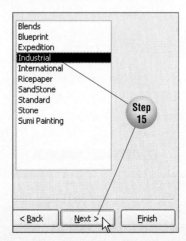

(16) Click Finish at the last Form Wizard dialog box to accept the default title of *Employee Benefits* and make sure *Open the form to view or enter information* is selected.

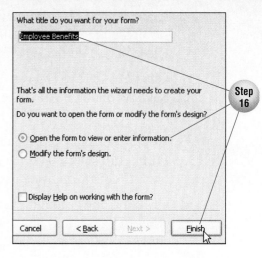

> In a few seconds the Employee Benefits form appears with the data displayed for record 1 as shown in Figure A3.3.

(17) Click the Next Record button to display record 2 in the form.

(18) Continue clicking the Next Record button to view several records using the form.

(19) Close the Employee Benefits form.

FIGURE A3.3 Employee Benefits Form

> When a relationship exists between two tables, a form can be created that includes fields from both tables. The related table is created as a *subform* of the primary table. In the next steps you will create a form and subform for the Employees and the Employee Expenses tables.

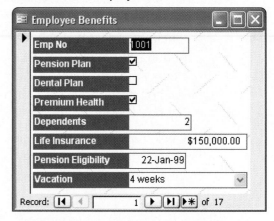

(20) With Forms still selected on the Objects bar, double-click *Create form by using wizard*.

(21) Click the down-pointing arrow at the right of the *Tables/Queries* text box and then click *Table: Employees* in the drop-down list.

(22) Add the following fields to the *Selected Fields* list box:
> *Emp No*
> *FirstName*
> *LastName*

(23) Click the down-pointing arrow at the right of the *Tables/Queries* text box and then click *Table: Employee Expenses* in the drop-down list.

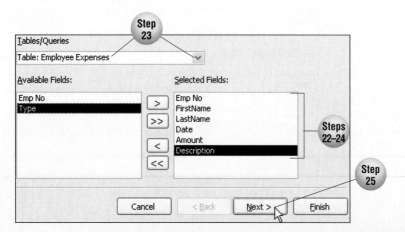

㉔ Add the following fields to the *Selected Fields* list box:
   Date
   Amount
   Description

㉕ Click Next.

㉖ Click Next at the second Form Wizard dialog box to accept the default options of viewing data *by Employees* and *Form with subform(s)*.

㉗ Complete the remaining steps in the Form Wizard as follows:
   • Accept the default layout of *Datasheet* for the subform.
   • Choose the *Blends* style.
   • Accept the default titles for the form and subform and open the form to view information.

   The form and subform appear as shown in Figure A3.4. Notice a separate Record Navigation bar exists for each form. The Record Navigation bar in the subform is used to scroll the records in the Employee Expenses table for the employee shown in the Employees form. The Record Navigation bar in the Employees form will move to the specified record in the Employees table and automatically display the related record(s) in the Employee Expenses table in the subform.

㉘ Click the Next Record button on the Record Navigation bar for the Employees form to view record 2. Notice the subform automatically changes to display the related record for Roman Deptulski in the Employee Expenses table.

FIGURE A3.4 Employees Form with Employee Expenses Subform

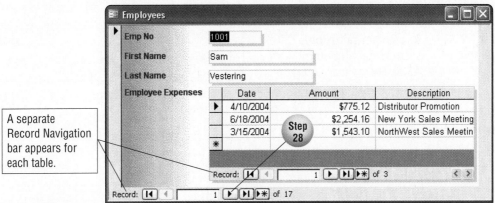

㉙ Continue clicking the Next Record button on the Record Navigation bar for the Employees form until you have viewed several employee names and related expense records.

㉚ Close the Employees form.

   Notice the two forms added to the Forms object list: *Employees* and *Employee Expenses Subform.* The subform is a separate object that can be viewed and/or edited separately from the Employees form; however, opening the Employees form will automatically open the Employee Expenses subform.

3.7 Modifying Controls in a Form

Once a form has been created using AutoForm or the Form Wizard, the form can be modified by opening it in Design view. A form is comprised of a series of objects referred to as *controls*. Each field from the table has a *label control* and a *text box control* placed side-by-side with the label control object placed first. The label control contains the field name and is used to describe the data that will be entered or viewed in the adjacent text box control. The text box control is the field placeholder where data is entered or edited. The controls can be moved, resized, formatted, or deleted from the form. A form's style which includes the color theme and fonts can be changed after the form has been created by opening the AutoFormat dialog box and selecting a different AutoFormat.

PROJECT: Some of the controls in the Employee Dates and Salaries form are wider than necessary for the data that will be entered or viewed. You will open the form in Design view, resize these controls, apply an AutoFormat to the form to improve its appearance, and change the font size of the controls on the form.

S T E P S

FIGURE A3.5 Employee Dates and Salaries Form Design View

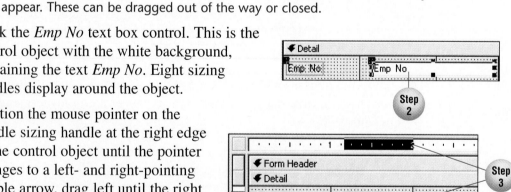

1. With **WEEmployees3** open and Forms still selected on the Objects bar, right-click *Employee Dates and Salaries,* and then click Design View at the shortcut menu. Maximize the window if it is not already maximized.

   A form contains three sections, as shown in Figure A3.5: Form Header, Detail, and Form Footer. The control objects for the fields in the table are displayed in the Detail section. A floating Toolbox displays in the window and a field list box may also appear. These can be dragged out of the way or closed.

2. Click the *Emp No* text box control. This is the control object with the white background, containing the text *Emp No*. Eight sizing handles display around the object.

3. Position the mouse pointer on the middle sizing handle at the right edge of the control object until the pointer changes to a left- and right-pointing double arrow, drag left until the right border is at position 2 on the horizontal ruler, and then release the left mouse button.

4. Resize the *Annual Salary* text box control to position 2 on the horizontal ruler by completing steps similar to those in Steps 2–3.

5. Resize the *Middle Initial* text box control to position 1.5 on the horizontal ruler by completing steps similar to those in Steps 2–3.

(6) Click in a gray area outside the form to deselect the Middle Initial control.

In the next step you will use the AutoFormat dialog box to change the form's style. Make sure no controls are selected before opening the AutoFormat dialog box or the new format will apply only to the selected control.

(7) Click the AutoFormat button [icon] on the Form Design toolbar.

(8) Click *International* in the *Form AutoFormats* list box and then click OK.

(9) Click Edit and then Select All.

All of the controls in the form are selected. You can also use the Shift key and click control objects to select multiple controls.

AutoFormat

Form AutoFormats:
Blends
Blueprint
Expedition
Industrial
International
Ricepaper
SandStone
Standard
Stone
Sumi Painting

Step 8

(10) Click the Properties button [icon] on the Form Design toolbar.

This opens the Multiple selection property sheet for the selected controls. Each control object in the form has a property sheet that can be used to change settings such as font, font size, color, and so on.

(11) Click the Format tab in the Multiple selection property sheet. Scroll down the property sheet, click in the *Font Size* property box, click the down-pointing arrow that appears, and then click *12* in the drop-down list.

(12) Close the Multiple selection property sheet.

(13) Click in the gray shaded area within the Form window to deselect the objects and then click the Save button.

(14) Click the View button [icon] on the Form Design toolbar to switch to Form view.

(15) With the first record in the table displayed in the form, click File, click Print, click *Selected Record(s)* in the *Print Range* section of the Print dialog box, and then click OK.

(16) Close the Employee Dates and Salaries form.

In Addition

Moving Control Objects

To move a selected control, position the mouse pointer on the border of the selected object until the pointer changes to a black hand and then drag the object to the desired location. Both the label and text box control move together. To move a text box or label control independently, drag the large black handle that appears in the top left corner of the control object.

Emp No   Emp No

Point to border to move both controls simultaneously.

Emp No   Emp No

Point to large black handle at top left corner to move control independently.

3.8 Adding Controls to a Form

The *Toolbox* that displays when the form is opened in Design view contains a palette of control object buttons that are used to add controls to a form. To add a control to a form, click the control object button in the Toolbox for the type of control you want to add, and then drag the outline of the object in the design grid the approximate height and width you want the control to be. Depending on the control object created, type the text or expression for the object and modify properties as required.

PROJECT: You will add label control objects that add descriptive text to the Employee Benefits form in the *Form Header* and *Form Footer* sections.

STEPS

(1) With **WEEmployees3** open and Forms still selected on the Objects bar, open the Employee Benefits form in Design view.

(2) Position the mouse pointer at the top of the gray *Detail* section border until the pointer changes to a black horizontal line with an up- and down-pointing arrow, drag the pointer down the approximate height shown at the right, and then release the mouse button.

PROBLEM? *Form Header/Form Footer* sections not visible? Click View and then click Form Header/Footer.

(3) Click the Label object button **Aa** in the Toolbox.

PROBLEM? Toolbox not visible? Click the Toolbox button on the Form Design toolbar.

(4) Position the crosshairs pointer with the label icon attached to it at the top left edge of the *Form Header* section, drag down to the approximate height and width shown at the right, and then release the mouse button.

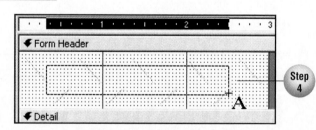

Label objects are used to add descriptive text, such as a heading, to a form. When the mouse button is released, a label box will appear with the insertion point at the top left edge of the box.

(5) Type **Employee Benefits** and then press Enter.

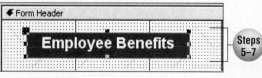

(6) With the label control object selected, click the Center button ≡ on the Formatting (Form/Report) toolbar. Click View, point to Toolbars, and then click Fomatting (Form/Report) if the toolbar is not visible.

⑦ With the label control still selected, click the *Font Size* list arrow on the Formatting (Form/Report) toolbar and then click *14* at the drop-down list.

⑧ Position the mouse pointer on the bottom of the gray *Form Footer* section border line until the pointer changes to a black horizontal line with an up- and down-pointing arrow, drag down until the *Form Footer* section is the approximate height shown below, and then release the mouse button.

⑨ Add a label control object to the *Form Footer* section as shown using the following specifications. *(Hint: Review Steps 3–7 if you need assistance creating this object.)*

- Substitute your first and last name for *Student Name*.
- Change the font size to *11* and click the Italics button on the Formatting (Form/Report) toolbar.

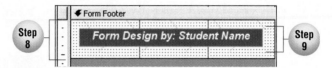

Step 8 | Form Footer — Form Design by: Student Name | Step 9

⑩ Click the Save button and then switch to Form view.

⑪ Print the selected record only.

⑫ Close the Employee Benefits form.

⑬ Open the Employees form in Design view.

⑭ Add a label control object to the right of *Emp No, First Name,* and *Last Name* in the *Detail* section as shown using the following specifications:

- Change the font size to *8* and center the text.
- Click the down-pointing arrow at the right of the *Fill/Back Color* option box and then click a pale yellow color square.
- Click the down-pointing arrow at the right of the *Line/Border Color* option box and then click a dark blue color square.

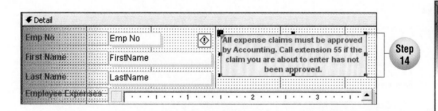

Detail — Emp No / First Name / Last Name / Employee Expenses — All expense claims must be approved by Accounting. Call extension 55 if the claim you are about to enter has not been approved. — Step 14

IN BRIEF

Add Controls to a Form

1 Open form in Design view.
2 Click control object button in Toolbox.
3 Drag control in design grid the approximate height and width desired.
4 Type text or expression as required.
5 Click Save button.

⑮ Click the Save button and then switch to Form view.

⑯ Print the selected record.

⑰ Close the Employees form.

3.9 Creating, Previewing, and Printing a Report

Information from the database can be printed while viewing tables in Datasheet view, while viewing a query results datasheet, or while browsing through forms by clicking the Print button on the toolbar. In these printouts all of the fields are printed in a tabular layout for datasheets or in the designed layout for forms. Create a report when you want to specify which fields to print and to have more control over the report layout and format. Access includes the Report Wizard, which generates the report based on selections made in a series of dialog boxes.

PROJECT: You will use the Report Wizard to create a report that will list the mailing addresses of the employees in a columnar format.

STEPS

1. With **WEEmployees3** open, click Reports on the Objects bar.

2. Double-click *Create report by using wizard.*

3. Click the down-pointing arrow at the right of the *Tables/Queries* text box and then click *Table: Employees* in the drop-down list.

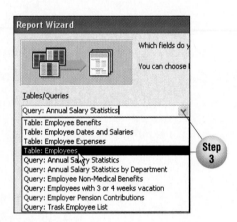

4. Click the Add All Fields button [>>] to move all of the fields in the Employees table from the *Available Fields* list box to the *Selected Fields* list box.

5. Click *Emp No* in the *Selected Fields* list box and then click the Remove Field button [<] to move *Emp No* back to the *Available Fields* list box.

6. Click *MiddleName* in the *Selected Fields* list box and then click the Remove Field button to move *MiddleName* back to the *Available Fields* list box.

7. Click Next.

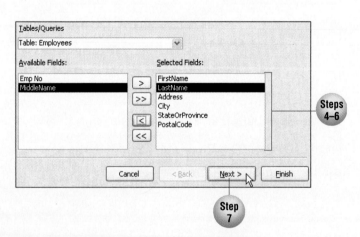

8 Click Next at the second Report Wizard dialog box to indicate that there is no grouping in the report.

> A grouping level in a report allows you to print records by sections within a table. For example, in an employee report you could print the employees grouped by city. In this example, you would double-click the *City* field to define the grouping level. The buttons with the up- and down-pointing arrows are used to modify the position of a field in the grouping level to increase or decrease its priority level if there is grouping by multiple fields.

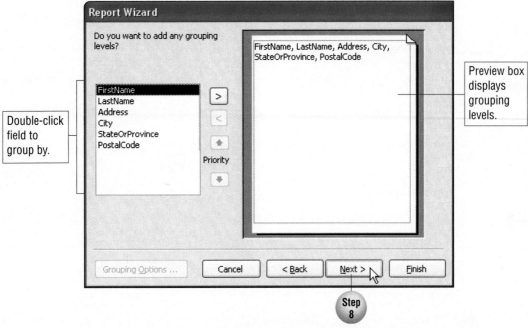

Double-click field to group by.

Preview box displays grouping levels.

Step 8

9 Click the down-pointing arrow next to the first text box in the third Report Wizard dialog box and then click *LastName* in the drop-down list.

> You can sort a report by up to four fields in the table.

Click here to change sort order from Ascending to Descending.

Step 9

10 Click Next.

11 Click *Columnar* in the *Layout* section in the fourth Report Wizard dialog box and then click Next.

> Use the preview box to view the selected layout before clicking the Next button.

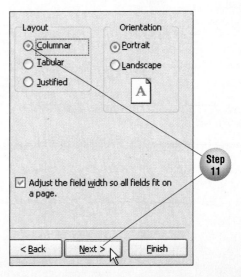

Step 11

(continued)

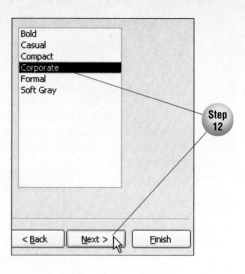

Step 12

12 Click *Corporate* in the style list box in the fifth Report Wizard dialog box and then click Next.

13 With *Preview the report* selected in the sixth Report Wizard dialog box, type **Employee Mailing Addresses** in the title text box and then click Finish.

> In a few seconds the report will appear in the Print Preview window.

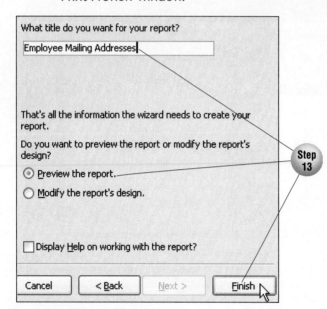

Step 13

14 Move the pointer (displays as a magnifying glass) to the middle of the report and then click the left mouse button.

> The zoom changes to *Fit* and the entire page is displayed in the Print Preview window, as shown in Figure A3.6.

FIGURE A3.6 Report Page in Print Preview

Entire first page displayed in Print Preview window.

⑮ Click the Next Page button ▶ on the Page navigation bar to display page 2 of the report.

⑯ Continue clicking the Next Page button until you have viewed all five pages in the report.

⑰ Click File and then Print.

⑱ Click *Pages* in the *Print Range* section.

⑲ With the insertion point positioned in the *From* text box, type **1** and then press Tab.

⑳ With the insertion point positioned in the *To* text box, type **1**.

Step 20

Step 18

Step 19

Step 21

㉑ Click OK.

In a few seconds, the first page only of the five-page *Employee Mailing Addresses* report will print.

㉒ Click the Close button on the Print Preview toolbar.

The Print Preview window closes and the report is displayed in Report Design view.

㉓ Close the Employee Mailing Addresses report.

In Addition

Creating a Report in Design View

A report can be created in a blank Design view window as shown below. Initially, the field list box is blank until a table or query is associated with the report. Double-click the Report Selector button to display the Report property sheet. Click the Data tab and then click the down-pointing arrow in the *Record Source* property box to select a table or query name. To add fields to the design grid, drag the field name from the field list box to the position in the grid where you want the field to appear.

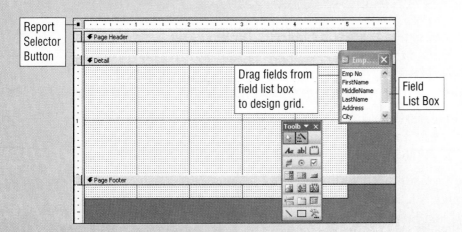

Report Selector Button

Drag fields from field list box to design grid.

Field List Box

Create a Report Using Report Wizard
1 Click Reports on Objects bar.
2 Double-click *Create report by using wizard.*
3 Choose table(s) and field(s) to include in report.
4 Click Next.
5 Choose grouping level(s) and click Next.
6 Choose field(s) to sort by and click Next.
7 Choose report layout and click Next.
8 Chose report style and click Next.
9 Type report title and click Finish.

3.10 Resizing and Moving Controls in a Report

Once a report has been created using the Report Wizard, the report can be modified by opening it in Design view. A report is similar to a form in that it is comprised of a series of objects referred to as controls. A report can be modified using similar techniques to those learned in Topics 3.7 and 3.8 on modifying and adding controls to a form.

PROJECT: After looking at the printout of the first page of the Employee Mailing Addresses report you decide that the space on the right side of the page is wasted. To reduce the number of pages required for the full report you will resize some controls, and move the *City*, *State/Province*, and *Postal Code* fields to the right side of the page.

S T E P S

① With **WEEmployees3** open and Reports selected on the Objects bar, open the Employee Mailing Addresses report in Design view.

A report contains five sections, as shown in Figure A3.7: Report Header, Page Header, Detail, Page Footer, and Report Footer. The control objects for the fields in the table are displayed in the *Detail* section. In a tabular report layout, the *Page Header* section contains the label control objects for the fields placed in the report. In Addition at the end of this topic explains the purpose of each report section.

FIGURE A3.7 Employee Mailing Addresses Report Design View

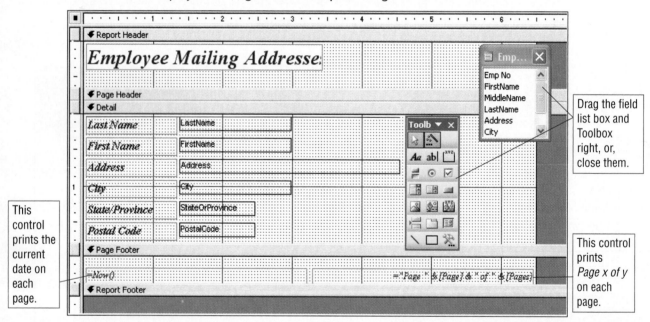

This control prints the current date on each page.

Drag the field list box and Toolbox right, or, close them.

This control prints *Page x of y* on each page.

② Click the *Address* text box control object to select it. This is the control with the black *Address* text.

Step 3

Step 4

③ Position the mouse pointer on the right middle sizing handle until the pointer displays as a left- and right-pointing arrow, drag left until the control is resized to position 3 on the horizontal ruler, and then release the mouse button.

④ Click the *City* text box control object. Hold down Shift and click the *StateOrProvince* text box control object. Hold down Shift and click the *PostalCode* text box control object.

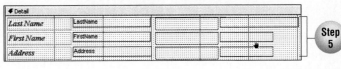

All three objects are now selected. Any actions performed while the objects are selected affect all three.

5 Position the mouse pointer over the border of any of the selected objects until the pointer displays as a black hand, drag the selected objects to the right of the *LastName* text box control as shown, and then release the mouse button.

Step 5

6 Click in a gray area outside the report to deselect the objects.

Moving the last three fields beside the first three will reduce the pages required for printing the mailing addresses since you are now using the full width of the page. In the next step you will reduce the size of the *Detail* section so that the space below *Address* where the fields were originally placed is not left blank on the printout.

7 Position the mouse pointer on the top of the gray *Page Footer* section border until the pointer changes to a black horizontal line with an up- and down-pointing arrow, drag the pointer up just below *Address* as shown, and then release the mouse button.

8 Click the Save button and then click the Print Preview button.

9 Click the Next Page button on the Page navigation bar to display page 2.

Step 7

Notice the report now requires only two pages.

10 Print the first page only of the report.

11 Close the Print Preview window and then close the Employee Mailing Addresses report. Click Yes when prompted to save changes to the report design.

12 Close the **WEEmployees3** database.

In Addition

Report Sections

The five sections of a report are described below.

Report Header:	Controls in this section are printed once at the beginning of the report.
Page Header:	Controls in this section are printed at the top of each page in the report.
Detail:	Controls in this section make up the body of the report.
Page Footer:	Controls in this section are printed at the bottom of each page in the report.
Report Footer:	Controls in this section are printed once at the end of the report.

IN BRIEF

Resize Control Objects
1 Open report in Design view.
2 Click object to be resized.
3 Drag sizing handles to increase or decrease size of object.
4 Click Save button.

Move Control Objects
1 Open report in Design view.
2 Click to select control to be moved.
3 Position pointer over border of selected control until pointer changes to black hand.
4 Drag control to desired location.
5 Click Save button.

FEATURES SUMMARY

Feature	Button	Menu	Keyboard
Aggregate functions	Σ	View, Totals	
AutoForm		Insert, Form, AutoForm	
Design View	⬰	View, Design View	
Form Header/Footer		View, Form Header/Footer	
Form View	⊞	View, Form View	
Form Wizard		Insert, Form, Form Wizard	
Property sheet	⬚	View, Properties	Alt + Enter
Report Wizard		Insert, Report, Report Wizard	
Run a query	!	Query, Run	
Select all controls		Edit, Select All	Ctrl + A
Simple Query Wizard		Insert, Query, Simple Query Wizard	
Toolbox	⚒	View, Toolbox	

PROCEDURES CHECK

Completion: In the space provided at the right, indicate the correct term or command.

1. This is the name of the wizard used to facilitate creating a query to select records from a table.
2. Type this entry in the *Annual Salary* criteria row in Query Design view to extract records of employees who earn more than $40,000.
3. Click the check box in this row in the query design grid to prevent a column from being displayed in the query results.
4. Click this button on the Query Design toolbar to add a new row to the design grid in which you can select statistical functions.
5. Use this method of creating a form if you want to choose the layout and style of the form.
6. The label control object button is located in this palette.
7. Click this button on the Form Design toolbar to change the formats of a selected control object.
8. Click this option in the Print dialog box to print only the active form.
9. A report is comprised of a series of objects referred to as this.

10. Provide the entry you would type in a blank *Field* row in the Query Design grid to calculate the total cost of an item given the following information:

- The total cost is calculated by multiplying the units ordered by the unit price.
- The units ordered is stored in a field named *UnitsOnOrder.*
- The unit cost is stored in a field named *UnitCost.*
- The new column should have the column heading *Total Cost.*

_____

List the names of the five sections found in a report.

11. _____   14. _____

12. _____   15. _____

13. _____

FIGURE A3.8

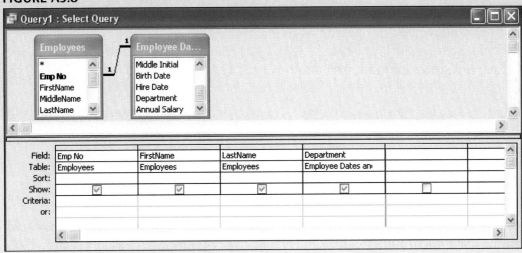

Use the Query Design window shown in Figure A3.8 to answer questions 16–18.

16. List the steps you would complete to sort the query results by the *LastName* field.

_____

_____

17. List the steps you would complete to add the field named *Annual Salary* in the Employee Dates and Salaries table to the blank column after *Department* in the query design grid.

_____

_____

18. List the steps you would complete to extract records of employees who work in the Overseas Distribution department.

_____

_____

_____

SKILLS REVIEW

Activity 1: CREATING A QUERY USING THE SIMPLE QUERY WIZARD

1 Open the **WEEmployees3** database.
2 Use the Simple Query Wizard to create a query that will display the fields from the Employees, Employee Dates and Salaries, and Employee Benefits tables as follows:

Employees	**Employee Dates and Salaries**	**Employee Benefits**
Emp No	*Hire Date*	*Life Insurance*
FirstName	*Annual Salary*	
LastName		

3 Accept the default Detail query and then type **Salaries and Life Insurance** as the title for the query.
4 View the query results datasheet.
5 Print the query results datasheet.
6 Close the Salaries and Life Insurance query.

Activity 2: SORTING A QUERY; ADDING A CRITERIA STATEMENT; CREATING A CALCULATED FIELD

1 With **WEEmployees3** open, open the Salaries and Life Insurance query in Design view.
2 Sort the query results by the *LastName* field in ascending order.
3 Add a criteria statement in the *Annual Salary* field that will extract the records of employees who earn more than $44,000. **(Hint: Numeric fields do not require quotation marks and should not include any currency symbols or commas.)**
4 Create a calculated field in the column after *Life Insurance* that will divide the *Annual Salary* column by 12 to display the monthly salary. Label the new column *Monthly Salary*.
5 Format the *Monthly Salary* column to display the calculated values in Currency format.
6 Use the Save As command to save the revised query as Employees Earning Over 44,000.
7 Run the query.
8 Preview and then print the query results datasheet.
9 Close the Employees Earning Over 44,000 query.

Activity 3: CALCULATING STATISTICS USING AGGREGATE FUNCTIONS

1 With **WEEmployees3** open, create a new query in Design view.
2 Add the Employee Expenses table to the design grid.
3 Add the *Amount* field to the design grid two times.
4 Display the *Total* row in the design grid.
5 Change the *Total* option in the first column to *Sum*.
6 Change the *Total* option in the second column to *Count*.
7 Change the caption property for the first column to *Total Expenses* and for the second column to *Number of Expense Claims*.
8 Save the query and name it Expense Statistics.
9 Run the query.

10　Best Fit the column widths in the query results datasheet.

11　Print and then close the Expense Statistics query, saving the changes.

Activity 4: CREATING A FORM USING THE FORM WIZARD; ENTERING RECORDS

1　With **WEEmployees3** open, create a new form for the Employee Expenses table using the following specifications:
- Add all of the fields in the Employee Expenses table to the form.
- Choose the *Columnar* layout.
- Choose the *Sumi Painting* style.
- Accept the default title for the form.

2　Add the following records to the Employee Expenses table using the form created in Step 1:

Emp No	1045	*Emp No*	1025
Date	5/13/05	*Date*	6/18/05
Amount	153.15	*Amount*	1127.88
Type	**Sales**	*Type*	**Sales**
Description	**Tradeshow**	*Description*	**Sales Conference**

3　Print all records in the table using the form.

4　Close the Employee Expenses form.

Activity 5: MODIFYING A FORM

1　With **WEEmployees3** open, open the Employee Expenses form created in Activity 4 in Design view.

2　Maximize the form window.

3　Expand the *Form Header* section approximately 1 inch and then insert the title *Expenses Form* in a label control object in the Form Header. Center the text in the label control object and then change the font size to 16 point.

4　Expand the *Form Footer* section approximately 1 inch and then insert the text *Form Design by: Student Name* in a label control object in the Form Footer. Substitute your first and last name for *Student Name*.

5　Decrease the width of the *Amount* text box control to position the right edge of the control at approximately 2.25 on the horizontal ruler.

6　Decrease the width of the *Type* text box control to position the right edge of the control at approximately 2.5 on the horizontal ruler.

7　Drag the right edge of the form (right edge of design grid) to approximately 3.5 on the horizontal ruler and then increase the width of the *Description* text box control to position the right edge of the control at approximately 3.25 on the horizontal ruler.

8　Switch to Form view.

9　Print the first record only in the form.

10　Close the Employee Expenses form, saving the changes.

Activity 6: CREATING A REPORT; RESIZING CONTROLS

1　With **WEEmployees3** open, use the Report Wizard to create a report based on the Salaries and Life Insurance query as follows:
- Add all of the fields from the query to the report.
- Do not include any grouping or sorting.

- Select the *Tabular* layout.
- Select the *Bold* style.
- Accept the default title for the report.

2 Preview and then print the report.
3 Display the report in Design view and then resize controls as follows:
- Drag the right edge of the *Last Name* label control object in the *Page Header* section to position 3 on the horizontal ruler.
- Drag the left edge of the *Hire Date* label control object in the *Page Header* section to approximately position 3.25 on the horizontal ruler.

4 Add your name in a label control object at the right side of the *Report Header* section.
5 Preview and then print the report.
6 Close the Salaries and Life Insurance report. Click Yes to save changes to the report design.
7 Close the **WEEmployees3** database.

PERFORMANCE PLUS

Assessment 1: CREATING A QUERY IN DESIGN VIEW; ADDING CRITERIA

1 The Bursary Selection Committee at Niagara Peninsula College would like you to provide them with the names of students who have achieved an A+ in all three of their courses.
2 Open **NPCGrades3**.
3 Create a query in Design view that will extract the records of those students who have an A+ in all three courses. Include student numbers, first names, last names, and grades. Sort the query in ascending order by student's last name. *(Hint: Type "A+" in the* **Criteria** *row to indicate the plus symbol is not part of an expression.)*
4 Save the query and name it A+ Students.
5 Run the query.
6 Best Fit the columns in the query results datasheet.
7 Print the query results datasheet in landscape orientation.
8 Close the A+ Students query.
9 Close **NPCGrades3**.

Assessment 2: CREATING A QUERY AND REPORT

1 Bobbie Sinclair, business manager of Performance Threads, would like a report that lists the costumes that were rented in August 2004.
2 Open **PTCostumeInventory3**.
3 Create a new query in Design view using the Costume Inventory table that will list the fields in the following order: *Costume No., Date Out, Date In, Character, Daily Rental Fee.*
4 Type the following criteria statement in the *Date Out* column that will extract the records for costumes that were rented in the month of August 2004:
Between August 1, 2004 and August 31, 2004
5 Expand the column width of the *Date Out* column to view the entire criteria statement.
6 Notice Access converted the long dates to short dates and added pound symbols to the dates in the criteria statement. Dates in Access queries are encased in pound symbols (#).

7   Sort the query results first by *Date Out*, then by *Date In*, and then by *Character* in ascending order.

8   Save the query and name it August 2004 Rentals.

9   Run the query. Close the query after viewing the query results datasheet.

10 Create a report based on the August 2004 Rentals query. Add all of the fields to the report. You determine the layout, style, and title for the report.

11 Add your name in a label object control at the right side of the *Report Header* section.

12 Preview and then print the report.

13 Close **PTCostumeInventory3**.

Assessment 3: CREATING AND MODIFYING A FORM

1   Staff at Performance Threads have mentioned that looking up a costume in the costume inventory datasheet is difficult, since there are so many records in the table. You decide to create a form for the staff in which they see only one record on the screen at a time as they are browsing the inventory.

2   Open **PTCostumeInventory3**.

3   Create a new form using the Form Wizard for the Costume Inventory table. You determine the layout, style, and title of the form. Include all of the fields in the form.

4   Modify the form as follows:
   • Add the title *Costume Inventory* in a label control object in the *Form Header*. You determine font size, color, and so on.
   • Add the text *Check for damage/repairs upon return* in a label control object in the *Form Footer*. You determine font size, color, and so on.
   • Resize the *Daily Rental Fee* text box control so that the right edge of the control aligns with the right edge of the *Date Out* and *Date In* objects below it.
   • Move and/or resize any other controls to improve the appearance of the form.

5   Change the font and font size of all of the control objects in the *Detail* section of the form to a font and size of your choosing. Resize controls if necessary after changing the font size.

6   Display the form in Form view.

7   Print the first record only in the form.

8   Close the form. Choose Yes to save changes to the form design.

9   Close **PTCostumeInventory3**.

Assessment 4: FINDING INFORMATION ON ADDING A PICTURE TO A FORM

1   Use the Help feature to find out how to insert a picture that doesn't change from record to record in a form. (***Hint: Start by typing*** add a picture to a form ***in the*** **Ask a Question** ***text box. Click the link*** Add a picture or object ***and then click the link in the Help window that describes how to use an image control to add an unbound picture.***)

2   Print the Help topic that you find.

3   Open **WEEmployees3**.

4   Open the Employee Expenses form in Design view.

5   Decrease the size of the label control object in the *Form Header* section so that the title requires only one-half of the width of the form.

6 Insert the company logo to the other half of the *Form Header* section. The logo file name is **Worldwide.jpg**. After inserting the JPEG file within the control object open the property sheet and then change the *Size Mode* property box to *Zoom*. Adjust the sizes of the objects in the *Form Header* section as necessary.

7 Print the first record only in the form.

8 Close the Employee Expenses form. Choose Yes to save the changes to the form design.

9 Close **WEEmployees3**.

Assessment 5: RESEARCHING TRAVEL DESTINATIONS ON THE INTERNET

1 You are considering taking a one-week vacation at the end of the term. The destination is flexible and will depend on available flights, costs, and activities.

2 Search the Internet for flight information to at least four destinations to which you might like to travel. Determine departure times, arrival times, and airfares for the week following the end of the current term.

3 Search the Internet for additional travel costs that you might incur for the destinations you used in Step 2. Include hotel accommodations, car rentals, and any tours or other activities that you might like to purchase.

4 Create a new database and name it **TravelDestinations** to store your travel data. Design and create a table within the database that will include all of the data you collected. *(Hint: If necessary, refer to Section 2, Performance Plus Assessment 7 for the steps on how to start a new blank database.)*

5 Design and create a form to be used to enter the data into the tables.

6 Enter data using the form created in Step 5.

7 Print all of the records in the form.

8 Close the form.

9 Close **TravelDestinations**.

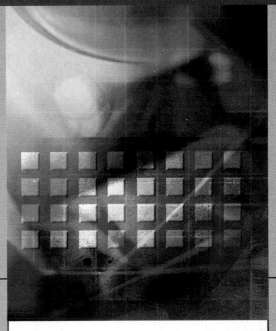

ACCESS SECTION 4

Modifying Tables and Reports, Performing Calculations, and Viewing Data

The structure of a table is modified by inserting, deleting, and moving fields. Filtering records allows the user to view a portion of the table data that meets a specific criterion. Access includes query wizards other than the Simple Query Wizard that assist with building queries for specific circumstances such as summarizing data, and finding duplicate or unmatched records in tables. Control objects can be created in which Access performs mathematical computations whenever a form or report is viewed or printed. Two views, PivotTable and PivotChart, are used to summarize and filter data. Tables and queries can be converted to a Web page to post on the Internet or a company's intranet by saving data in a data access page. Once a database contains several objects, it can be difficult to track the source from which objects are derived or are dependent. Display the Object Dependencies task pane to help with finding these associations. In this section you will learn the skills and complete the projects described here.

Note: Before beginning this section, delete any existing databases on your disk and copy each database as needed. Remember to remove the read-only attribute from each database after copying. If necessary, refer to page 1 for instructions on how to remove the read-only attribute. If necessary, check with your instructor before deleting any database files.

Skills

- Insert and delete fields in a table
- Move a field in a table
- Apply and remove filters to a table
- Create a crosstab query
- Create a find unmatched query
- Create a find duplicates query
- Create a calculated control object in a form and report
- Use align and spacing options in a form and report to improve the layout
- Move and resize control objects in a report
- Modify properties of form and report controls
- Summarize data in a PivotTable
- Summarize data in a PivotChart
- Save a table and a query as a Web page
- View a list of objects within a database
- View dependencies for an object
- Create a new database using a database wizard

Projects

Move, insert, and delete fields in tables; filter records; create queries to total field values grouped by two fields; create queries to find the records in a related table with no match in the primary table; use a query to find duplicate records; modify a form and report to include a calculated control; summarize and filter data in a PivotTable and PivotChart; save a table and query as a Web page; view a list of objects and associations between objects; create a new database in which to store contact information; create and modify a report.

Filter records of students who achieved A+ in a course.

The *Waterfront Bistro*

Modify the structure of the Inventory List table; filter records by a supplier code; create a query and PivotChart; create a

Performance Threads
Theatrical Fabrics,
Costumes and Supplies

Modify a form for browsing the costume inventory to include a calculation that will display the

4.1 Inserting, Deleting, and Moving Fields

Display a table in Design view to insert or delete fields or to reposition a field. In a previous section, you learned how to move columns in Datasheet view for sorting purposes. Although the column can be moved in the datasheet, the position of the field in the table structure will remain where it was originally created unless the field is moved in Design view. Exercise caution when making changes to the table structure after records have been entered. Data in deleted fields will be lost and existing records will have null values in new fields that have been added. As a precaution it is a good idea to make a backup of the database before making structural changes.

PROJECT: After consultation with Rhonda Trask, human resources manager of Worldwide Enterprises, you realize that the three name fields in the Employee Dates and Salaries table are redundant since the same fields also exist in the Employees table. You will delete these fields, add a new field for annual performance review dates, and reposition the *Annual Salary* field.

STEPS

1. Open **WEEmployees4**.

2. Open the Employee Dates and Salaries table in Design view.

3. Click the insertion point in any text in the *Last Name* row.

4. Click the Delete Rows button ⊒ in the Table Design toolbar.

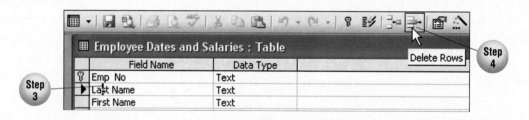

Step 3 / Step 4 / Delete Rows

5. Click Yes at the Microsoft Office Access message asking you to confirm that you want to permanently delete the selected field(s) and all of the data in the field(s).

   Multiple fields can be deleted in one operation. In the next step, you will select both the *First Name* and *Middle Initial* fields, and in Step 7 you will delete both fields at the same time.

6. Position the mouse pointer in the field selector bar for the *First Name* field until the pointer changes to a right-pointing black arrow, and then drag the pointer down until both the *First Name* and *Middle Initial* fields are selected.

7. Click the Delete Rows button on the Table Design toolbar.

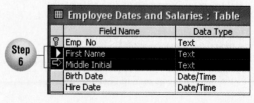

Step 5 / Step 6

⑧ Click Yes at the Microsoft Office Access message.

⑨ Click the insertion point in any text in the *Department* row.

New rows are inserted *above* the active field.

⑩ Click the Insert Rows button  on the Table Design toolbar.

The new row is positioned between the *Hire Date* and *Department* fields.

⑪ Type **Review Date** in the *Field Name* column and then change the data type to *Date/Time*.

⑫ Move the mouse pointer in the field selector bar beside *Annual Salary* until the pointer changes to a right-pointing black arrow and then click the left mouse button to select the field.

Step 11	Employee Dates and Salaries : Table	
	Field Name	Data Type
🔑	Emp No	Text
	Birth Date	Date/Time
	Hire Date	Date/Time
▶	Review Date	Date/Time ▾
	Department	Text
	Annual Salary	Currency

Step 13 / Step 12	Employee Dates and Salaries : Table	
	Field Name	Data Type
🔑	Emp No	Text
	Birth Date	Date/Time
	Hire Date	Date/Time
	Review Date	Date/Time
	Department	Text
▶	Annual Salary	Currency

⑬ With the pointer still positioned in the field selector bar beside *Annual Salary* (pointer now displays as a white arrow), drag the pointer up between the *Birth Date* and *Hire Date* fields, and then release the left mouse button.

As you drag the mouse, a black line appears between existing field names, indicating where the selected field will be repositioned when the mouse button is released and the white arrow pointer displays with a gray shaded box attached to it.

⑭ Click in any field to deselect the *Annual Salary* row and then click the Save button.

⑮ Switch to Datasheet view.

⑯ Print and then close the Employee Dates and Salaries table.

In Addition

Adding Data in a New Field

Consider the following tips for entering data in the datasheet for a new field that has been inserted into a table after several records have already been created.

- Click in the new column (e.g., *Review Date*) in the first row of the table, type the data for the new field, and then press the Down Arrow key to remain in the same column for the next record.

- Press Ctrl + ' (apostrophe) if the data for the current record is the same field value as the data in the field immediately above the current record. Microsoft Access will automatically duplicate the entry that is above the active field.

IN BRIEF

Delete a Field
1 Open table in Design view.
2 Select field(s) to be deleted.
3 Click Delete Rows button on Table Design toolbar.
4 Click Yes.
5 Click Save button.

Insert a Field
1 Open table in Design view.
2 Click in field row immediately below where new field is to be located.
3 Click Insert Rows button on Table Design toolbar.
4 Type field name, assign data type, and modify properties as needed.
5 Click Save button.

Move a Field
1 Open table in Design view.
2 Select and then drag field to new location.
3 Click Save button.

4.2 Applying and Removing Filters

A *filter* is used to view only those records in a datasheet that meet specified criteria. For example, you might want to view only those records of employees who work in a specific department. Once the filter has been applied, you can view, edit, and print the filtered records. The records that do not meet the criteria are temporarily removed from the datasheet. Click the Remove Filter button on the Table Datasheet toolbar to redisplay all records in the table. Records can be filtered using two methods—***Filter By Selection***, and ***Filter By***

Form. The difference between a filter and a query is that the query can be saved for future use, whereas the filter has to be redone each time.

PROJECT: You will use the Filter By Selection method in the Employee Dates and Salaries table to display and print records of employees who work in the European Distribution department. In the Employee Benefits table, you will use the Filter By Form method to print a list of employees who receive four weeks of vacation.

STEPS

1. With **WEEmployees4** open, open the Employee Dates and Salaries table in Datasheet view.

2. Select the text *European Distribution* in the *Department* column in the third row of the datasheet.

Step 2

Department
North American Distribution
Overseas Distribution
European Distribution
North American Distribution
North American Distribution

3. Click the Filter By Selection button 🏷 on the Table Datasheet toolbar.

   Only records of employees in the European Distribution department are displayed, as shown in Figure A4.1. Notice the word *(Filtered)* appears after the number of records on the Record Navigation bar at the bottom of the datasheet.

FIGURE A4.1 Filtered Datasheet

Emp	Birth Date	Annual Salary	Hire Date	Review Date	Department
+ 1010	12/10/1952	$69,725.00	1/30/1999		European Distribution
+ 1035	2/4/1970	$44,694.00	3/15/2001		European Distribution
+ 1045	6/18/1961	$42,238.00	4/12/2001		European Distribution
+ 1050	5/9/1967	$44,387.00	2/9/2002		European Distribution
+ 1060	1/6/1964	$42,126.00	6/22/2003		European Distribution
+ 1080	1/8/1978	$43,659.00	1/17/2004		European Distribution
*		$0.00			

Employee Dates and Salaries : Table

4. Print the table.

5. Click the Remove Filter button 🏷 on the Table Datasheet toolbar.

   All records in the table are redisplayed.

6. Close the Employee Dates and Salaries table. Click No if prompted to save changes.

7. Open the Employee Benefits table in Datasheet view.

8. Click the Filter By Form button 🏷 on the Table Datasheet toolbar.

   All records are temporarily removed from the datasheet and a blank row appears. Specify the field value in the field by which you want to filter by using the drop-down lists in the fields in the blank row. The Table Datasheet toolbar is replaced by the Filter/Sort toolbar.

⑨ Click in the *Vacation* column, click the down-pointing arrow that appears, and then click *4 weeks* in the drop-down list.

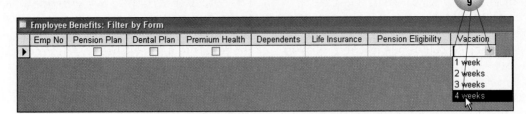

Step 9

⑩ Click the Apply Filter button ![filter] on the Table Datasheet toolbar.

> The Apply Filter button changes to the Remove Filter button once a filter has been applied to a table.

Step 10

Emp No	Pension Plan	Dental Plan	Premium Health	Dependents	Life Insurance	Pension Eligibility	Vacation
1001	☑	☐	☑	2	$150,000.00	22-Jan-99	4 weeks
1015	☑	☑	☑	2	$199,999.00	17-Nov-99	4 weeks
1020	☑	☐	☐	0	$100,000.00	03-Feb-01	4 weeks
1025	☑	☑	☑	1	$150,000.00	01-Jun-01	4 weeks
*	☑	☐	☐	0	$0.00		

Employee Benefits : Table

⑪ Change the page orientation to landscape and then print the table.

⑫ Click the Remove Filter button on the Table Datasheet toolbar.

> All records in the table are redisplayed.

⑬ Close the Employee Benefits table. Click No if prompted to save changes.

In Addition

Filtering by Multiple Criteria

The Filter By Form window contains a tab labeled *Or* at the bottom of the window (shown at the right), just above the Status bar. Use this tab to filter by more than one criterion. For example, you could display records of employees who receive three weeks or four weeks of vacation. To do this, click the Filter By Form button and select *3 weeks* in the *Vacation* field, click the Or tab, and then select *4 weeks* in the *Vacation* field in the second form. Click the Apply Filter button. Records that meet either the three weeks or four weeks criterion will be displayed.

Use this tab to add a second criterion to filter by.

IN BRIEF

Filter By Selection
1 Open table in Datasheet view.
2 Select field value in field you want to filter by.
3 Click Filter By Selection button.
4 View, print, and/or edit data as required.
5 Click Remove Filter button.

Filter By Form
1 Open table in Datasheet view.
2 Click Filter By Form button.
3 Click in field you want to filter by.
4 Click down-pointing arrow and click value you want to filter by.
5 Click Apply Filter button.
6 View, print, and/or edit data as required.
7 Click Remove Filter button.

4.3 Summarizing Data Using a Crosstab Query

A *crosstab query* calculates aggregate functions such as sum and avg in which field values are grouped by two fields. A wizard is included that guides you through the steps to create the query. The first field selected causes one row to display in the query results datasheet for each group. The second field selected displays one column in the query results datasheet for each group. A third field is specified that is the numeric field to be summarized. The intersection of each row and column holds a value that is the result of the specified aggregate function for the designated row and column group. For example, suppose you want to find out the total sales achieved by each salesperson by state. Each row in the query results could be used to display a salesperson's name with the state names in columns. Access summarizes the total sales for each person for each state and shows the results in a spreadsheet-type format.

PROJECT: Worldwide Enterprises has been in an expansion phase in the last seven years and has been hiring aggressively to keep up with growth. Rhonda Trask wants to find out the salary cost that has been added to the payroll each year by department. You will use a crosstab query to calculate the total value of annual salaries for new hires in each year by each department.

STEPS

① With **WEEmployees4** open, click Queries on the Objects bar and then click the New button on the Database window toolbar.

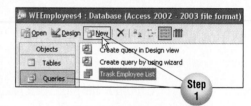

Step 1

② Click *Crosstab Query Wizard* in the New Query list box and then click OK.

The fields that you want to use for grouping must all exist in one table or query. In situations where the fields that you want to group by are in separate tables, you would first create a new query that contains the fields you need and then start the crosstab query wizard. In your project, all three fields that you need are in one table.

③ If necessary click *Tables* in the *View* section of the first Crosstab Query Wizard dialog box and then click *Table: Employee Dates and Salaries*.

Step 3

④ Click Next.

In the second Crosstab Query Wizard dialog box you choose the field in which the field's values become the row headings in the query results datasheet.

⑤ Double-click *Department* in the *Available Fields* list box to move the field to the *Selected Fields* list box and then click Next.

At the next dialog box you choose the field in which the field's values become the column headings in the query results datasheet.

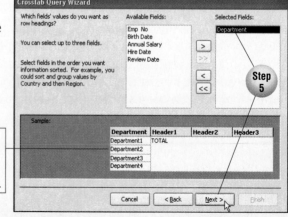

Sample section previews the query results as you make each selection.

Step 5

(6) Click *Hire Date* in the field list box and then click Next.

> Whenever a date/time field is chosen for the column headings, Access displays a dialog box asking you to choose the time interval to summarize by with the default option set to *Quarter*.

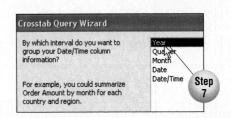

(7) Click *Year* in the list box and then click Next.

> The final field to be selected is the numeric field to be summarized and the aggregate function to be used to calculate the values.

(8) Click *Annual Salary* in the *Fields* list box and then click *Sum* in the *Functions* list box.

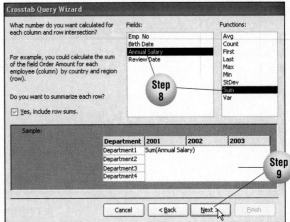

(9) Look at the datasheet layout displayed in the *Sample* section of the Crosstab Query Wizard and then click Next.

(10) Type **New Hire Payroll Costs by Department by Year** in the *What do you want to name your query?* text box and then click Finish.

> The query results datasheet displays as shown in Figure A4.2. Notice a total column is inserted next to each department name with the total broken down to show the amount for each year that makes up each department's payroll cost.

FIGURE A4.2 Crosstab Query Results Datasheet

Department	Total Of Annual	1998	1999	2000	2001	2002	2003	2004
European Distribution	$286,829.00		$69,725.00		$86,932.00	$44,387.00	$42,126.00	$43,659.00
North American Distribution	$249,521.00	$69,725.00	$90,543.00	$45,558.00			$43,695.00	
Overseas Distribution	$287,820.00	$69,725.00	$42,824.00		$45,395.00	$42,248.00		$87,628.00

(11) Best Fit each column's width.

(12) Display the Page Setup dialog box and change the left and right margins to 0.5 inch and the page orientation to landscape.

(13) Print the query results datasheet.

(14) Close the New Hire Payroll Costs by Department by Year query. Click Yes to save changes to the layout.

IN BRIEF

Create a Crosstab Query
1 Click Queries on Objects bar.
2 Click New button.
3 Click Crosstab Query Wizard and click OK.
4 Choose table or query name and click Next.
5 Choose field for row headings and click Next.
6 Choose field for column headings and click Next.
7 Choose numeric field to summarize and function to calculate and click Next.
8 Type query name and click Finish.

4.4 Using a Query to Find Unmatched Records

A *find unmatched query* is used when you want Access to compare two tables and produce a list of the records in one table that have no matching record in the other related table. This type of query is useful to produce lists such as customers who have never placed an order or an invoice with no payment record. Access provides the Find Unmatched Query Wizard that builds the select query by guiding the user through a series of dialog boxes.

PROJECT: You will create a find unmatched query to make sure that you have entered a record in the Employee Benefits table for all employees at Worldwide Enterprises.

S T E P S

1. With **WEEmployees4** open and Queries selected on the Objects bar, click the New button on the Database window toolbar.

2. Click *Find Unmatched Query Wizard* in the New Query list box and then click OK.

> At the first dialog box in the Find Unmatched Query Wizard you choose the table or query in which you want to view records in the query results datasheet. If an employee is missing a record in the benefits table you will need the employee's number and name which is in the Employees table.

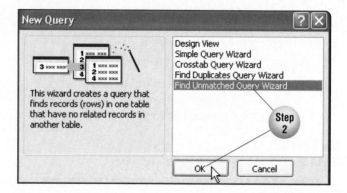

3. With *Tables* selected in the *View* section of the first Find Unmatched Query Wizard dialog box, click *Table: Employees* and then click Next.

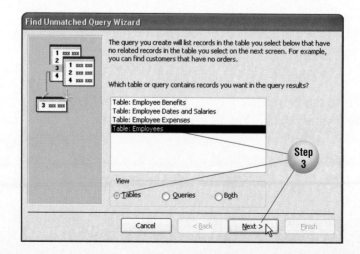

④ With *Table: Employee Benefits* already selected in the table list box, click Next.

> In order for Access to compare records you need to specify the field in each table that would have matching field values.

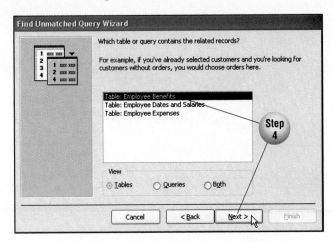

⑤ With *Emp No* already selected in the *Fields in 'Employees'* and *Fields in 'Employee Benefits'* list boxes, click Next.

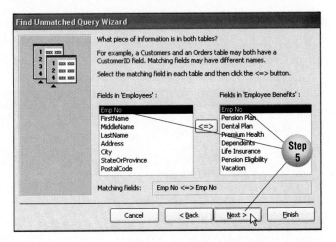

⑥ At the fourth Find Unmatched Query Wizard dialog box, double-click *Emp No, FirstName,* and *LastName* to move the fields from the *Available fields* list box to the *Selected fields* list box below *What fields do you want to see in the query results?* and then click Next.

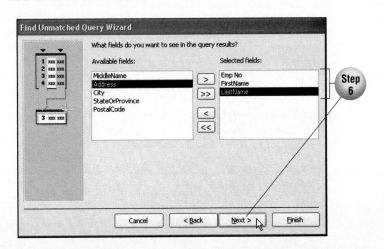

(continued)

7 Click Finish at the last Find Unmatched Query Wizard dialog box to accept the default name of *Employees Without Matching Employee Benefits* and *View the results* option.

> The query results datasheet opens with four records displayed showing the four employees that are missing a record in the benefits table.

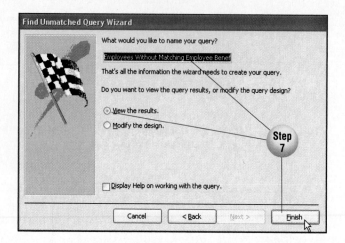

8 Look at the records displayed in the query results datasheet. Access has found four records in the Employees table for which no matching record exists in the Employee Benefits table.

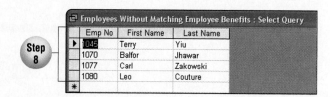

9 Print the query results datasheet.

10 Close the Employees Without Matching Employee Benefits query.

11 Click Tables on the Objects bar and then open the Employee Benefits table in Datasheet view.

12 Add the following records to the Employee Benefits table.

> You are adding records for employee numbers 1045, 1070, and 1080 only. You suspect an error has occurred in the Carl Zakowski record which you will explore in the next topic.

Emp No	1045
Pension Plan	Yes
Dental Plan	No
Premium Health	Yes
Dependents	1
Life Insurance	100000
Pension Eligible	10-Oct-01
Vacation	2 weeks

Emp No	**1070**
Pension Plan	Yes
Dental Plan	Yes
Premium Health	Yes
Dependents	**3**
Life Insurance	**195000**
Pension Eligible	**22-May-05**
Vacation	1 week
Emp No	**1080**
Pension Plan	Yes
Dental Plan	No
Premium Health	No
Dependents	**0**
Life Insurance	**50000**
Pension Eligible	**17-Jul-04**
Vacation	1 week

13 Change the page orientation to landscape and then print the Employee Benefits datasheet.

14 Close the Employee Benefits table.

15 Click Queries on the Objects bar.

In Addition

Design View for a Find Unmatched Query

The dialog boxes in the Find Unmatched Query Wizard assist with creating a Select Query that searches the records in the related table for null field values in the field specified as common to both tables. *Null* is the term used for a field in which the field value is blank, or empty. The design view for the Employees Without Matching Employee Benefits is shown below. Notice the entry in the criteria row for the *Emp No* field from the Employee Benefits table is *Is Null.*

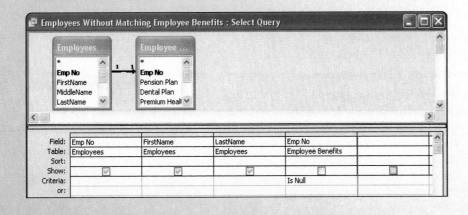

IN BRIEF

Create a Find Unmatched Query

1 Click Queries on Objects bar.
2 Click New button.
3 Click Find Unmatched Query Wizard and click OK.
4 Choose table or query to display in query results and click Next.
5 Choose related table or query and click Next.
6 Choose matching field in each table field list and click Next.
7 Choose fields you want to view in query results and click Next.
8 Type query name and click Finish.

4.5 Using a Query to Find Duplicate Records

A *find duplicates query* searches a specified table or query for duplicate field values within a designated field or fields. Create this type of query if you suspect a record, such as a product record, has inadvertently been entered twice under two different product numbers. Other examples of applications for this type of query are included in the In Addition section following this topic. Access provides the Find Duplicates Query Wizard that builds the select query based on the selections made in a series of dialog boxes.

PROJECT: You suspect that someone who filled in for you last week while you were away at a conference added an employee record to the Employees table in error. You will use a find duplicates query to check for this occurrence in the Employees table.

S T E P S

1 With **WEEmployees4** open and Queries selected on the Objects bar, click the New button on the Database window toolbar.

2 Click *Find Duplicates Query Wizard* in the New Query list box and then click OK.

> At the first dialog box in the Find Duplicates Query Wizard you choose the table or query in which you want Access to look for duplicate field values.

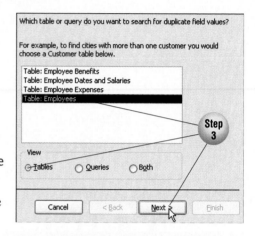

3 With *Tables* selected in the *View* section of the first Find Duplicates Query Wizard dialog box, click *Table: Employees* and then click Next.

> At the second Find Duplicates Query Wizard dialog box you choose the fields that may contain duplicate field values. Since *Emp No* is the primary key field in the Employees table you know that it is not possible for an employee record to be duplicated using the same employee number, therefore, you will use the name fields to check for duplicates.

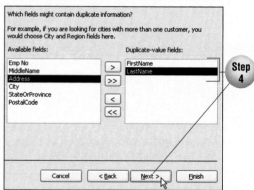

4 Double-click *FirstName* and *LastName* to move the fields from the *Available fields* list box to the *Duplicate-value fields* list box and then click Next.

5 Move all of the fields from the *Available fields* list box to the *Additional query fields* list box and then click Next.

> If an employee record has been duplicated you would want to see all of the fields to ensure that the information in both records is exactly the same. If not, you would need to check which record contains the accurate information before deleting the duplicate.

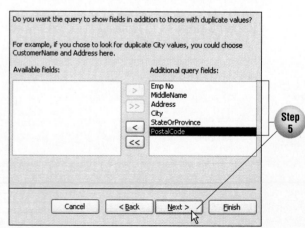

⑥ Click Finish at the last dialog box to accept the default name *Find duplicates for Employees* and *View the results* option.

> The query results datasheet displays showing that Carl Zakowski has two records in the Employees table under two different employee numbers.

	First Name	Last Name	Emp No	Middle Name	Address	City	State/Province	Postal Code
▶	Carl	Zakowski	1077	Waylon	65 Dyer Avenue	New York	NY	10110-
	Carl	Zakowski	1050	Waylon	65 Dyer Avenue	New York	NY	10110-
✱								

Step 6

⑦ Change the page orientation to landscape and then print the query results datasheet.

⑧ Move the mouse pointer in the record selector bar next to the first record (with *Emp No 1077*) until the pointer changes to a right-pointing black arrow, right-click, and then click Delete Record at the shortcut menu.

Step 8

First Name	Last Name	Emp No	Middle
...kowski	1077	Waylon
...kowski	1050	Waylon

New Record
Delete Record
Cut

⑨ Click Yes to confirm the record deletion.

⑩ Close the Find duplicates for Employees query.

⑪ Double-click *Find duplicates for Employees* in the query list. The query result now displays a blank datasheet. Since you deleted the duplicate record for Carl Zakowski in Step 8, duplicate records no longer exist in the Employees table.

⑫ Close the Find Duplicates for Employees query.

In *Addition*

More Examples for Using a Find Duplicates Query

In this topic you used a find duplicates query to locate and then delete an employee record that was entered twice. A find duplicates has many other applications. Consider the following examples:

- Find the records in an Orders table with the same customer number so that you can identify who your loyal customers are.
- Find the records in a Customer table with the same last name and mailing address so that you send only one mailing to a household to save on printing and postage costs.
- Find the records in an Employee Expenses table with the same employee number so that you can see which employee is submitting the most claims.

IN BRIEF

Create a Find Duplicates Query
1 Click Queries on Objects bar.
2 Click New button.
3 Click Find Duplicates Query Wizard and click OK.
4 Choose table or query to search for duplicates and click Next.
5 Choose the field(s) that might contain duplicate field values and click Next.
6 Choose additional fields to display in query results and click Next.
7 Type query name and click Finish.

4.6 Adding a Calculated Control to a Form; Using Align and Spacing Controls

Add a text box control object to a form to perform calculations. Formulas are based on existing fields in the table similar to the method used to calculate in queries. A calculated control is not stored as a field—each time the form is opened, the results are dynamically calculated. The align options *Left, Right, Top,* and *Bottom* are used to arrange selected objects at the same horizontal or vertical position on a form or report. The spacing between controls can be adjusted using the Horizontal Spacing and Vertical Spacing options on the Format menu. The spacing can be increased, decreased, or made even.

PROJECT: Worldwide Enterprises pays its employees 4% of their annual salary as vacation pay each year. You will add a control object to the Employee Dates and Salaries form to calculate the vacation pay entitlement for each employee and use align and spacing options to improve the layout of the form.

STEPS

① With **WEEmployees4** open, click Forms on the Objects bar, and then open the Employee Dates and Salaries form in Design view.

② Maximize the form window if it is not already maximized.

③ Position the mouse pointer at the top of the gray *Form Footer* section border and then drag the *Form Footer* section down the approximate height shown.

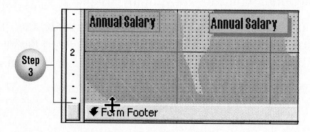

④ Click the Text Box object button ⬚abl⬚ in the Toolbox.

⑤ Position the crosshairs pointer with the text box icon attached to it below the *Annual Salary* text box control, drag to create the object the approximate height and width shown below, and then release the mouse button.

A text box label control object and an unbound control object box appear. An **unbound control** contains data that is not stored anywhere. A control that displays a field value in a table is referred to as a **bound control** since the object contents are bound to the table.

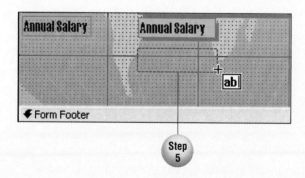

6 Click in the unbound text box control.

> An insertion point appears so that you can type the formula. A mathematical expression in a text box control begins with the equals sign (=) and field names are encased in square brackets.

7 Type **=[Annual Salary]*0.04** and then press Enter.

> Do not be concerned if a portion of the formula is not visible within the control object. The entire formula is stored in the object's property sheet as the **Data Source.** In Form view, the object will be displaying the calculated values, not the formula.

The number displayed in your label control may vary.

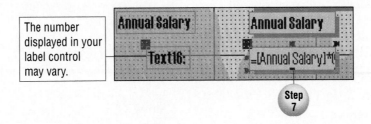

Step 7

8 Right-click over the calculated control object and then click Properties at the shortcut menu.

9 Click the Format tab in the Text Box property sheet. With the insertion point positioned in the *Format* property box, click the down-pointing arrow that appears, scroll down the drop-down list, and then click *Currency.*

10 Scroll down the Format property sheet, click in the *Font Size* property box, click the down-pointing arrow that appears, and then click *12* in the drop-down list.

11 Close the Text Box property sheet.

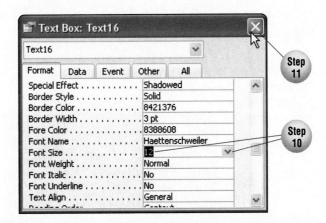

Step 11

Step 10

12 Click the label control object adjacent to the text box control (currently displays *Text##* [where ## is the number of the label object]) to select it.

(continued)

13 Click a second time inside the selected label control object to display the insertion point, delete the current text, type **Vacation Pay**, and then press Enter.

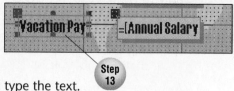

Step 13

The width of the box will increase as you type the text.

14 With the *Vacation Pay* label control still selected, hold down the Shift key and then click the *Annual Salary* label control above *Vacation Pay*.

15 Click Format, point to Align, and then click Left.

Align Left arranges the left edges of the controls with the left edge of the leftmost control in the selected group.

Steps 14–15

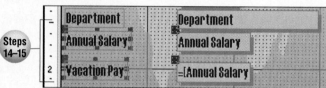

16 Click in a gray area to deselect the *Annual Salary* and *Vacation Pay* label objects.

17 Position the white arrow pointer at the top left of the *Detail* section (just below the *Detail* section border and not on an individual object) and then drag a selection rectangle around all of the control objects within the section.

Use the mouse to select multiple objects by dragging a rectangle when the number of objects to be changed is numerous and using Shift + click would be tedious.

Step 17

18 With all objects in the *Detail* section selected, click Format, point to Vertical Spacing, and then click Make Equal.

The vertical space between the selected objects is now evenly distributed. The position of the highest control does not change.

Step 18

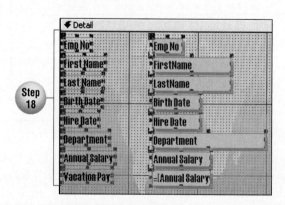

19 Click in a gray area to deselect the objects.

20 Change the text in the label control object in the *Form Footer* section to insert your name in place of *Student Name*.

21 Click the Save button and then switch to Form view.

22 With the record for employee number 1001 displayed, click in the *Last Name* field, and then click the Sort Ascending button $\begin{bmatrix} A \\ Z \end{bmatrix}$ on the Form View toolbar.

> The record for employee number 1015, Lyle Besterd displays. You can now scroll the records alphabetically by employee last name.

23 Print the selected record only and then close the Employee Dates and Salaries form, saving changes.

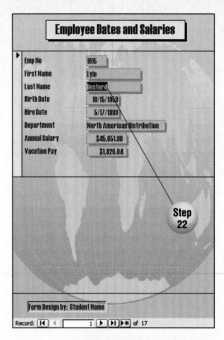

In Addition

Error Checking in Access

Automatic error checking for common types of errors in forms and reports is turned on by default in Access 2003. When Access determines that an error has occurred, a small green diagonal triangle appears in the upper left corner of the control. Click the control with an error indicator to display the Error Checking Options button. Pointing to the Error Checking Options button displays a ScreenTip indicating the type of error that has occurred. Click the Error Checking Options button to choose from a list of options with which you can correct the error. In the example shown below an equals sign is missing at the beginning of the mathematical expression in the calculated control. To correct the error, click *Edit the Control's Control Source Property* at the Error Checking Options drop-down menu. The property sheet for the calculated control opens with an insertion point active in the Control Source property box. Add the equals sign and close the property sheet. The Error Checking indicator will be removed once the error is corrected.

IN BRIEF

Add a Calculated Control Object to a Form
1 Open form in Design view.
2 Click Text Box object button in Toolbox.
3 Drag control in design grid the approximate height and width desired.
4 Click in Unbound control object and type formula.
5 Change format properties for unbound control as required.
6 Type desired label in text box label control.
7 Click the Save button.

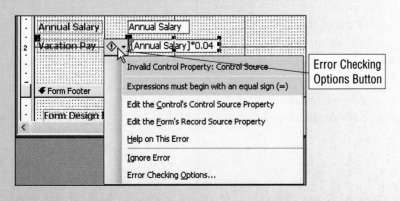

4.7 Modifying a Report; Creating a Calculated Control

Modifying a report by resizing, moving, aligning, spacing, and formatting controls is often required to fine-tune the appearance after the Report Wizard creates the report. A calculated control object can be created in a report by completing steps similar to those learned in the previous topic. As in a form, the calculations are not stored in the table, but are dynamically calculated each time the report is previewed or printed.

PROJECT: Worldwide Enterprises estimates that it incurs benefit costs of an additional 22% of an employee's annual salary to pay for the benefit plans it offers to employees. You will create a report to print a list of employees based on a query, add a control to calculate the estimated benefit cost, and then modify the report.

STEPS

1 With **WEEmployees4** open, click Reports on the Objects bar and then create a new report using the Report Wizard as follows.

- Add all fields from the Trask Employee List query.
- Double-click the *Department* field in the second Report Wizard dialog box to group the entries in the report by department.
- Sort the report by *LastName* in ascending order.
- Choose the block layout in landscape orientation.
- Choose the soft gray style.
- Type **Employee Benefit Cost** as the title of the report.

2 Click the Close button on the Print Preview toolbar after viewing the report to display the report in Design view.

> This report contains an additional section named *Department Header* since the report is grouped by the *Department* field.

3 Maximize the report window if it is not already maximized.

4 Click the *Emp No* label control in the *Page Header* section.

5 Hold down the Shift key and then click *Emp No* in the *Detail* section.

> Both controls are now selected.

6 Press Delete.

7 Click the *Last Name* label control in the *Page Header* section, Shift + click *LastName* in the *Detail* section, and then resize the right edge of either control to position 3 on the horizontal ruler.

> With both controls selected, dragging the right sizing handle of one control will also resize the other control.

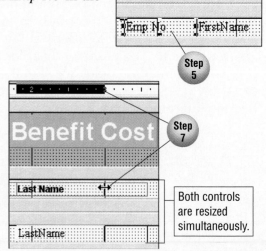

⑧ Select both *First Name* controls. Position the mouse pointer on the border of one of the selected controls until the pointer changes to a black hand, and then drag the controls left to align the left edge at position 3.25 on the horizontal ruler.

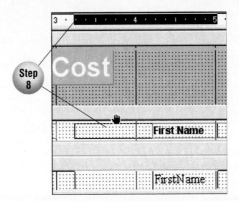

⑨ With both *First Name* controls still selected, resize the right edge of either control to position 4.25 on the horizontal ruler.

⑩ Select both *Hire Date* controls and then drag the border of either control left to align the left edge at position 4.5 on the horizontal ruler.

⑪ Select both *Annual Salary* controls and then drag the border of either control left to align the left edge at position 5.5 on the horizontal ruler.

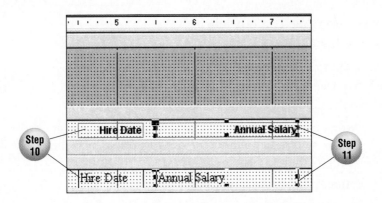

⑫ If necessary, scroll right until you can see the right edge of the report.

⑬ Click the Label object button **Aa** in the Toolbox.

PROBLEM?

Click 🔨 on the Report Design toolbar if the Toolbox palette is not visible.

(continued)

(14) Position the crosshairs with the label icon attached in the *Page Header* section to the right of *Annual Salary*, drag to create the outline the approximate height and width shown, and then release the mouse button.

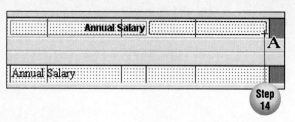

Step 14

(15) Type **Estimated Benefit Cost** and then press Enter.

(16) Click the *Annual Salary* control in the *Page Header* section, click the Format Painter button on the Report Design toolbar, and then click the *Estimated Benefit Cost* label control. Widen the control if necessary to display the entire label contents.

> Format Painter copies the formatting attributes for the *Annual Salary* label to the *Estimated Benefit Cost* label.

(17) Click the Text Box object button ab| in the Toolbox.

(18) Position the crosshairs with the text box icon attached in the *Detail* section below the *Estimated Benefit Cost* label, drag to create an object the same height and width as the label, and then release the mouse button.

(19) Click in the text box control (displays *Unbound*), type **=[Annual Salary]*0.22**, and then press Enter.

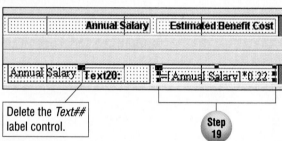

Delete the *Text##* label control.

Step 19

(20) Click the label control to the left of the text box control (displays *Text##* [where ## is the text box label number]) and press Delete.

(21) Click the Print Preview button to preview the report. If necessary, scroll right to view the right edge of the report where the calculated values display.

> Notice that the calculated values are aligned at the left edge of the column, do not display a consistent number of decimal places, and the border lines are not surrounding the values as in the remainder of the report.

(22) Close the Print Preview window.

(23) Click the *Annual Salary* control in the *Detail* section, click the Format Painter button, and then click the control object containing the mathematical expression.

> The border attributes are copied to the calculated control object.

(24) Right-click the calculated control object, and then click Properties at the shortcut menu.

(25) Change the following properties on the Format tab in the property sheet and then close the property sheet.

- Format property to *Currency*
- Text Align property to *Right*

(26) Preview the Employee Benefit Cost report. Close the Print Preview window and if necessary, adjust controls by moving and/or resizing objects to improve the report's appearance. Make sure all text is entirely visible within the report.

> PROBLEM ?
>
> Click Format and then Snap to Grid to turn off the snapping feature if you are having difficulty resizing or moving an object a small distance. Snapping means the control will jump to the nearest grid point when you release the mouse.

27 Click the Save button.

28 Click the Sorting and Grouping button 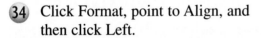 on the Report Design toolbar.

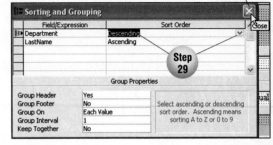

Display the Sorting and Grouping dialog box to make changes to the report's grouping and sort order after the report has been created. In this report, *Department* is shown first with the grouping icon in the field selector bar since the report is grouped and sorted first by the department name and then sorted by the *LastName* field.

29 Click in the *Sort Order* column next to *Department*, click the down-pointing arrow that appears, and then click *Descending*.

30 Close the Sorting and Grouping dialog box.

31 Create a label object at the right side of the *Report Header* section with the text *Report by: Student Name*. Substitute your name for *Student Name*.

32 Create another label object below your name in the *Report Header* section with the text *Benefits calculated at 22% of Annual Salary*. Resize the control if necessary so that the text does not wrap to a second line.

Your vertical spacing may vary depending on where the two label controls were originally situated.

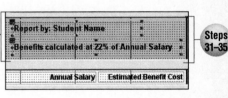

Steps 31–35

33 Select both label controls created in Steps 31 and 32.

34 Click Format, point to Align, and then click Left.

35 With both label controls still selected, click Format, point to Vertical Spacing, and then click Increase.

36 Click the Save button and then preview the report in the Print Preview window.

37 Print and then close the Print Preview window.

38 Close the Employee Benefit Cost report.

In Addition

Form, Report, and Section Properties

A property sheet is available for each form, report, and for each section within a form or report. Open the property sheets to change formats, control page breaks, and so on. To display the property sheet for a form or report, double-click the Form or Report Selector button ▣ at the top left corner of the horizontal and vertical rulers in Design view. Double-click the gray section bar to display the property sheet for a section.

IN BRIEF

Modify Report Control Properties
1 Display report in Design view.
2 Click control object to be modified.
3 Change properties as required.
4 Save changes.
5 Preview report.

4.8 Summarizing Data Using PivotTable View

A PivotTable is an interactive table that organizes and summarizes data based on the fields you designate for row headings, column headings, and source record filtering. Aggregate functions such as sum, avg, and count are easily added to the table using the AutoCalc button on the PivotTable toolbar. A PivotTable provides more options for viewing data than a crosstab query because you can easily change the results by filtering data by an item in a row, a column, or for all source records. This interactivity allows you to analyze the data for numerous scenarios. PivotTables are easily created using a drag-and-drop technique in PivotTable view.

PROJECT: The accountant for Worldwide Enterprises wants a report that illustrates the expenses by type submitted by employees in the North American Distribution department. You will begin by creating a query since the required information is in more than one table and then use a PivotTable to summarize the data.

S T E P S

1 With **WEEmployees4** open, click Queries on the Objects bar and then create a new query in Design view as follows.
- Add the Employees, Employee Dates and Salaries, and Employee Expenses tables to the design grid.
- Add the following fields in order: *FirstName, LastName, Department, Date, Type,* and *Amount.*
- Save the query and name it Expenses for PivotTable.

2 Run the query to view the query results datasheet.

3 Click View and then click PivotTable View.

> The datasheet changes to PivotTable layout with four sections and a PivotTable Field List box. Dimmed text in each section describes the type of fields that should be dragged and dropped.

4 Click LastName in the PivotTable Field List box, drag the field to the section labeled *Drop Row Fields Here* until a blue border outlines the section, and then release the mouse.

> When you release the mouse, a row for each field value in the *LastName* field appears with the caption *Last Name* and a filter arrow at the top of the list.

5 Click *Type* in the PivotTable Field List box, drag the field to the section labeled *Drop Column Fields Here* until a blue border outlines the section, and then release the mouse.

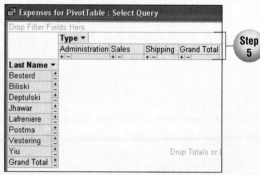

> A column for each field value in the field named *Type* appears with the caption **Type** and filter arrow above the list.

6 Click *Department* in the PivotTable Field List box and then drag the field to the section labeled *Drop Filter Fields Here*.

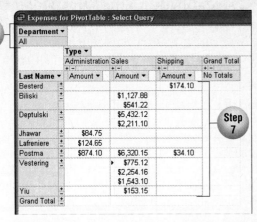

Step 6

Step 7

7 Click *Amount* in the PivotTable Field List box and then drag the field to the section labeled *Drop Totals or Detail Fields Here*.

> Access summarizes and arranges the data within the columns and rows.

8 Click one of the *Amount* column headings.

> All cells in the table containing values from the *Amount* field are selected as indicated by the light blue color.

9 Click the AutoCalc button $\Sigma\blacktriangledown$ on the PivotTable toolbar and then click *Sum* at the drop-down list.

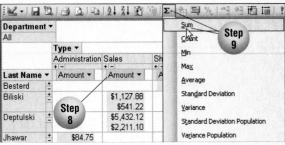

Step 9

Step 8

> Each employee's expenses are subtotaled and the Grand Totals are now calculated. A *Totals* field showing the *Sum of Amount* function is added to the PivotTable Field List box.

10 Click the filter arrow (black down-pointing arrow) to the right of *Department*.

11 Click the *(All)* check box to deselect all department names, click the *North American Distribution* check box, and then click OK.

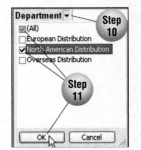

Step 10

Step 11

> The PivotTable hides all data except those employees in the North American Distribution department.

12 Right-click over the *Sum of Amount* column heading and then click Properties at the shortcut menu.

13 Click the Captions tab in the Properties sheet, click in the *Caption* text box, delete *Sum of Amount,* and then type **Total Expenses**.

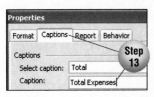

Step 13

14 Click the Format tab, click the Bold button, click the *Fill Color* arrow next to *Background color,* click a light blue color square, and then close the Properties sheet.

15 Right-click over the *Grand Total* row heading, click Properties at the shortcut menu, click the Format tab, click the Red Font Color button in the *Text format* section, and then close the Properties sheet.

Step 16

Step 15

16 Change the font color of the values in the *Grand Total* column by completing steps similar to those in Step 15.

17 Click the Save button. Change the left margin to 1.5 inches and then print the PivotTable.

18 Close the Expenses for PivotTable query.

4.9 Summarizing Data Using PivotChart View

A PivotChart performs the same function as a PivotTable with the exception that the source data is displayed in a graph instead of a table. A chart is created by dragging fields from the Chart Field List box to the *Filter, Data, Category,* and *Series* sections of the chart. By default, the Sum function is used to total the summarized data. To change to a different function, click the Sum of [Field name] button, click the AutoCalc button on the PivotChart toolbar, and then click the desired function in the drop-down

list. As with a PivotTable, the PivotChart can be easily altered using the filter arrows.

PROJECT: After reviewing the table prepared in Topic 4.8, the accountant has asked for two more reports in chart form. You will display the Expenses for PivotTable query in a PivotChart, modify the filter and chart settings, and then print the PivotCharts.

S T E P S

① With **WEEmployees4** open and Queries selected on the Objects bar, open the Expenses for PivotTable query in Datasheet view.

② Click View and then click PivotChart View.

    The information created in the PivotTable in the last topic is automatically graphed in a column chart with filter buttons for *Department, Last Name,* and *Type.*

③ Click the Field List button 📋 on the PivotTable toolbar to close the Chart Field List box.

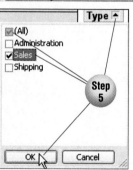

④ Click the *Department* filter arrow (blue down-pointing arrow), click the *(All)* check box, and then click OK.

    The chart is updated to reflect expense claims in all departments.

⑤ Click the *Type* filter arrow, click the *(All)* check box to deselect all types, click the *Sales* check box, and then click OK.

    The chart is updated to reflect only sales expense claims for all departments.

⑥ Right-click *Axis Title* at the bottom of the chart and then click Properties at the shortcut menu.

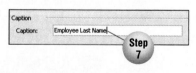

⑦ Click the Format tab in the Properties sheet, click in the *Caption* text box, delete the existing text, type **Employee Last Name**, and then close the Properties sheet.

⑧ Change the vertical *Axis Title* at the left side of the chart to *Sales Expenses* by completing steps similar to those in Steps 6–7.

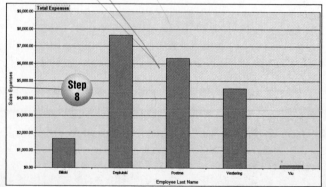

⑨ Click the Save button.

⑩ Change the page orientation to landscape and then print the PivotChart.

⑪ Click View and then click PivotTable View.

> Notice the PivotTable is dynamically linked to the PivotChart. Changes made to the filter settings in Chart view are also updated in Table view.

⑫ Click the *Department* filter arrow, click the *North American Distribution* check box to deselect the department, and then click OK.

> The PivotTable updates to reflect expenses for all departments except North American Distribution.

⑬ Click View and then click PivotChart.

⑭ Print the revised PivotChart.

⑮ Click the Save button and then close the Expenses for PivotTable query.

Department ▾			
All			
	Type ▾		
		Sales	Grand Total
		+ −	+ −
Last Name ▾		Amount ▾	Total Expenses
Biliski	+ −	$1,127.88	$1,669.10
		$541.22	
		$1,669.10	
Deptulski	+ −	$5,432.12	$7,643.22
		$2,211.10	
		$7,643.22	
Postma	+ −	$6,320.15	$6,320.15
		$6,320.15	
Vestering	+ − ▸	$775.12	$4,572.38
		$2,254.16	
		$1,543.10	
		$4,572.38	
Yiu	+ −	$153.15	$153.15
		$153.15	
Grand Total	+ −	$20,358.00	$20,358.00

Step 11

In Addition

Creating a PivotChart from Scratch

In this topic, a PivotChart was automatically created when you selected PivotChart View because an existing PivotTable was saved with the query. When you open a table or query without an existing PivotTable and choose PivotChart View, the screen looks like the one shown at the right. Drag the fields from the PivotChart Field List box to the appropriate sections in the chart. You will create a PivotChart from scratch in a Performance Plus assessment at the end of this section.

In BRIEF

Create a PivotChart
1 Open desired table or query in datasheet view.
2 Click View, PivotChart View.
3 Drag field for X-axis categories from Chart Field List to *Drop Category Fields Here*.
4 Drag field to use for filtering data from Chart Field List to *Drop Filter Fields Here*.
5 Drag field(s) with data to be graphed to *Drop Data Fields Here*.
6 Change axis titles as required.
7 Filter data as required.
8 Click Save.

4.10 Creating Data Access Pages

Data access pages are Web pages created from tables or queries that are used for interacting with Microsoft Access databases on the Internet or on a company's intranet. Data access pages are stored outside the database file. Designing and modifying a data access page is similar to designing forms and reports. Access includes a Page Wizard that can be used to create a data access page.

PROJECT: You will create a Web page that will enable employees to view their benefits through a Web browser.

STEPS

1. With **WEEmployees4** open, click Pages on the Objects bar.

2. Double-click *Create data access page by using wizard*.

3. With *Table: Employee Benefits* already selected in the *Tables/Queries* list box in the first Page Wizard dialog box, double-click *Emp No* in the *Available Fields* list box to move the field to the *Selected Fields* list box.

4. Double-click *Pension Plan, Dental Plan, Premium Health, Life Insurance,* and *Vacation* to move the fields from the *Available Fields* list box to the *Selected Fields* list box.

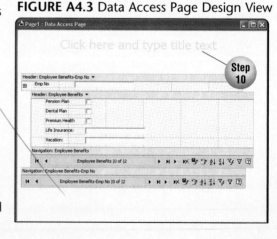

5. Click Next.

6. Click Next at the second Page Wizard dialog box to continue without adding a grouping level to the page.

7. Click Next at the third Page Wizard dialog box to continue without specifying a field to sort the records by.

8. Click Finish at the last Page Wizard dialog box to accept the default title *Employee Benefits* and *Modify the page's design*.

    In a few seconds the data access page is displayed in Design view, as shown in Figure A4.3.

FIGURE A4.3 Data Access Page Design View

9. Close the Field List task pane and the Toolbox and then maximize the Data Access Page window.

10. Click over the text *Click here and type title text* and then type **Worldwide Enterprises Employee Benefits**.

    As soon as you click over *Click here and type title text*, the text will disappear and will be replaced with the text you type.

11. Click Format and then Theme.

    A *theme* is a group of predefined formats and color schemes for bullets, fonts, horizontal lines, background images, and other data access page elements.

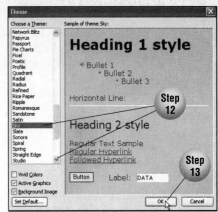

12 Scroll down the *Choose a Theme* list box and then click *Sky*.

> The selected theme's colors, bullet style, line style, text and hyperlinked text style, button style, and text box formats display in the *Sample of the theme Sky* section.

13 Click OK.

14 Click the Save button on the Page Design toolbar.

15 Type **WEEmployeeBenefits** in the *File name* text box and then click Save. (If a message appears stating that the connection string of this page specifies an absolute path and might not be able to connect to data through the network, click OK.)

16 Click File and then Web Page Preview.

> The data access page displays in the default Web browser window.

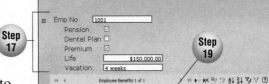

17 Click the plus symbol next to employee number *1001* in the Web browser window.

> The record expands to display the benefits associated with employee number 1001.

18 Click File on the Web browser Menu bar and then click Print.

19 Scroll through a few of the records in the data access page in the Web browser window by clicking the Next Record button on the lower navigation bar and then expanding the record by clicking the plus symbol.

20 Close the Web browser window.

21 Close the WEEmployeeBenefits Data Access Page window.

In Addition

More about Data Access Pages

When a data access page is created, Access creates a folder in which to store the Web page files. Although the Web pages are not stored directly within the database, the data access page is directly connected to the source database. When a user displays the data access page in the browser, she or he is viewing a copy of the page. Any filtering or sorting that is done to affect the way the data is *displayed* affects only this copy of the page. Changes made to the *content* of the data, however, such as inserting, editing, or deleting field values, are updated immediately in the source database so that everyone viewing the data access page is working with the same information.

Create a Data Access Page

1. Click Pages on Objects bar.
2. Double-click *Create data access page by using wizard*.
3. Choose table or query and field(s) to include in Web page.
4. Click Next.
5. Choose a grouping level and click Next.
6. Choose a field to sort by and click Next.
7. Type page title and click Finish.
8. Modify page in Design view as required.
9. Click Save.
10. Type Web page file name, click Save.

4.11 Viewing Objects and Object Dependencies

As you have learned throughout this book, the structure of a database is comprised of table, query, form, and report objects. Tables are related to other table(s) by creating one-to-one, one-to-many, or many-to-many relationships. Queries, forms, and reports draw the source data from records in the tables to which they have been associated and forms and reports can include subforms and subreports, which further expand the associations between objects. A database with a large number of interdependent objects is more complex to work with. Viewing a list of the objects within a database and viewing the dependencies between objects can be beneficial to ensure an object is not deleted or otherwise modified causing an unforeseen affect on another object. Access provides two features that provide information on objects: Database Properties and the Object Dependencies task pane.

PROJECT: You will view a list of objects in the WEEmployees4 database and then view the other objects dependent on a table in the Object Dependencies task pane.

STEPS

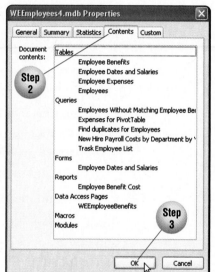

1. With **WEEmployees4** open, click File and then click Database Properties.

2. Click the Contents tab in the WEEmployees4.mdb Properties dialog box.

3. Review the list of objects within the *Document contents* list box and then click OK.

4. Click Tables on the Objects bar and then click *Employee Dates and Salaries*.

5. Click View and then click Object Dependencies to open the Object Dependencies task pane.

   By default, *Objects that depend on me* is selected and the task pane lists the names of objects for which the Employee Dates and Salaries table is the source. Next to each object in the task pane list is an expand button (plus symbol). Clicking the expand button will show objects dependent at the next level. For example, if a query is based upon the Employee Dates and Salaries table and the query is used to generate a report, clicking the expand button next to the query name would show the report name.

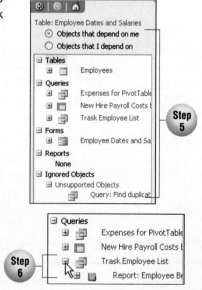

6. Click the expand button (plus symbol) next to the <u>Trask Employee List</u> link in the *Queries* list in the Object Dependencies task pane.

   The object expands to show that the Trask Employee List is used to generate the report named Employee Benefit Cost.

7. Click *Objects that I depend on* at the top of the Object Dependencies task pane.

   The objects in the task pane list change to illustrate the names of other objects in the database for which Employee Dates and Salaries is dependent upon.

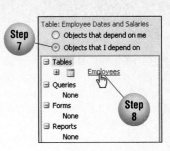

8 Position the mouse pointer over the table named Employees in the Object Dependencies task pane until the name displays as a hyperlink and then click the left mouse button.

> Clicking an object name in the Object Dependencies task pane opens the object in Design view. Tables which have a relationship defined are shown as dependent objects in the expanded Tables list. Deleting a relationship in the Relationships window removes the dependency between tables. See In Addition at the end of this topic for information on deleting relationships.

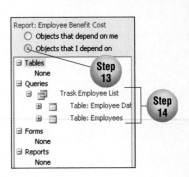

9 Close the Employees : Table window.

10 Close the Object Dependencies task pane.

11 Click Reports on the Objects bar and then click the Employee Benefit Cost report.

12 Click View and then click Object Dependencies.

13 Click *Objects that I depend on* at the top of the Object Dependencies task pane.

14 If necessary, expand the Trask Employee List query name.

> The expanded list shows that the Trask Employee List is derived from two tables: Employee Dates and Salaries and Employees.

15 Close the Object Dependencies task pane.

16 Close the **WEEmployees4** database.

In Addition

Deleting Relationships between Tables

To delete a relationship between tables, open the Relationships window, right-click the black join line between the table names, and then click Delete at the shortcut menu. A dialog box will appear asking you to confirm that you want to permanently delete the relationship from the database.

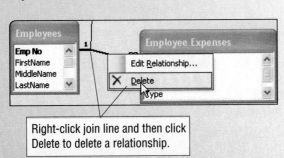

Right-click join line and then click Delete to delete a relationship.

IN BRIEF

View Database Objects
1 Click File, Database Properties.
2 Click Contents tab.
3 Review list of objects in list box.
4 Click OK.

View Object Dependencies
1 Click to select object name for which you want to view dependencies.
2 Click View, Object Dependencies.
3 Choose either *Objects that depend on me or Objects that I depend on.*
4 Expand items in list as desired.
5 Close Object Dependencies task pane.

4.12 Creating a New Database Using a Wizard

Access provides database wizards that can be used to create new database files. The wizards include a series of dialog boxes that guide you through the steps of creating the database by selecting from predefined tables, fields, screen layouts, and report layouts. When the database is created, a Main Switchboard window displays on the Access screen in place of the Database window. The Main Switchboard is a special type of form that contains options used to access the various objects generated by Access. The Main Switchboard form is automatically displayed each time the database is opened.

PROJECT: You will create a new database to store contact information for Worldwide Enterprises using the Contact Management Wizard.

STEPS

1. Click the New button 🗋 on the Database toolbar.

2. Click the <u>On my computer</u> link in the *Templates* section of the New File task pane.

Step 2

3. Click the Databases tab in the Templates dialog box and then double-click *Contact Management* in the *Databases* list box.

Step 3

4. Type **WEContacts** in the *File name* text box in the File New Database dialog box and then click Create.

5. Click Next at the first Database Wizard dialog box that contains information about the type of data the database will store.

6. Click Next at the second Database Wizard dialog box to accept the default fields in the tables.

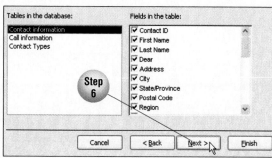

Step 6

Access displays the predefined tables in the *Tables in the database* list box. For each table, a set of predefined fields are displayed in the *Fields in the table* list box. Fields displayed in italics are not created by default but can be included by clicking the check box next to the field name.

7. Click *Industrial* as the screen display style in the third Database Wizard dialog box and then click Next.

8. Click *Bold* for the report style in the fourth Database Wizard dialog box and then click Next.

9. Click Finish at the last Database Wizard dialog box to accept the default title of *Contact Management* for the database.

The Database Wizard creates the tables, forms, and reports for the new database. A progress box displays indicating the tasks Access is completing. When the database is complete, Access opens the Main Switchboard window that is used to access the various components of the new database.

10. Click *Enter/View Contacts* in the Main Switchboard window.

11. Type the data in the first record as shown in Figure A4.4.

12. Click the button for Page 2 at the bottom of the record.

13. Type **sgrey@emcp.net** in the *Email Name* field.

14. Close the Contacts form.

15. Click *Preview Reports* in the Main Switchboard window.

16. Click *Preview the Alphabetical Contact Listing Report.*

17. Click the Print button on the Print Preview toolbar and then click the Close button.

18. Click *Return to Main Switchboard* in the Reports Switchboard window.

19. Click Tools, Options, and then click the General tab in the Options dialog box.

20. Click the *Compact on Close* check box and then click OK.

21. Click *Exit this database* in the Main Switchboard window.

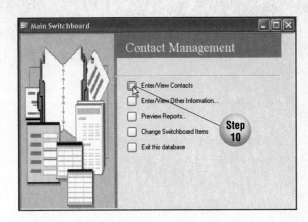

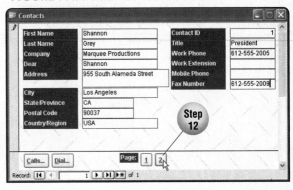

FIGURE A4.4 Data for First Record

In Addition

Closing the Main Switchboard

Click the Close button on the Main Switchboard title bar if you need to work with the objects in the Database window. A minimized title bar with the name of the database will be positioned just above the Status bar. Click the Maximize or Restore button on the Database title bar to restore the Database window. Tables or other objects can be customized by opening them in Design view and making the required changes. To return to the Main Switchboard after closing it, click Forms on the Objects bar, and then double-click *Switchboard*.

IN

BRIEF

Create a New Database Using a Wizard

1 Click New button.

2 Click On my computer link in New File task pane.

3 Click Databases tab in Templates dialog box and double-click desired database wizard.

4 Type database file name and click Create.

5 Click Next.

6 Select fields to include in each table and click Next.

7 Select screen layout and click Next.

8 Select report style and click Next.

9 Type title for database and click Finish.

FEATURES SUMMARY

Feature	Button	Menu	Keyboard
Align controls on form or report		Format, Align, Left, Right, Top, or Bottom	
Crosstab query		Insert, Query, Crosstab Query Wizard	
Database Wizard		File, New	Ctrl + N
Delete rows		Edit, Delete Rows	
Filter by form		Records, Filter, Filter By Form	
Filter by selection		Records, Filter, Filter By Selection	
Find Duplicates Query Wizard		Insert, Query, Find Duplicates Query Wizard	
Find Unmatched Query Wizard		Insert, Query, Find Unmatched Query Wizard	
Horizontal spacing in form or report		Format, Horizontal Spacing	
Insert rows		Insert, Rows	
Object dependencies		View, Object Dependencies	
Page Wizard		Insert, Page, Page Wizard	
PivotChart view		View, PivotChart View	
PivotTable view		View, PivotTable View	
Property sheet		View, Properties	Alt + Enter
Theme		Format, Theme	
Toolbox		View, Toolbox	
Vertical spacing in form or report		Format, Vertical Spacing	

PERFORMANCE PLUS

Completion: In the space provided at the right, indicate the correct term or command.

1. To move, insert, or delete a field in a table, open the table in this view. _____

2. Click this button on the Datasheet toolbar to temporarily remove all records from the display and then select a criterion from a drop-down list of field values in a field. _____

3. Start this query wizard to sum data in a field that is grouped by two fields. _____

4. Use this query wizard to produce a datasheet showing names and telephone numbers from the Customer table for those customers who have no record in the Order table. _____

5. Click this button in the Toolbox to create a calculated field in a form or report. _____

6. Use this option to position multiple controls at the leftmost edge of the selected group in Design view for a form or report. _____

7. This is the name of the view in which you can create an interactive table that organizes and summarizes data based on fields you drag and drop for row and column headings. _____

8. This is the name of the wizard used to facilitate creating a Web page for a table or query. _____

9. This is the name given to a group of predefined formats and color schemes that can be applied to Web pages. _____

10. Open this task pane to find out which other objects are based upon the selected object. _____

Identify the following features represented by the buttons:

11. _____

12. _____

13. _____

14. _____

15. _____

16. _____

SKILLS REVIEW

Activity 1: MOVING AND DELETING FIELDS; MODIFYING FIELD PROPERTIES

1 Open the **WEEmployees4** database.
2 Open the Employee Expenses table in Design view.
3 Move the *Amount* field between the *Emp No* and *Date* fields.
4 Delete the *Type* field.
5 Save the table.
6 Switch to Datasheet view.
7 Print the datasheet.
8 Select the word *Sales* in the *Description* column of any record and then use Filter by Selection to view sales-related expenses.
9 Print the filtered datasheet.
10 Remove the filter and then close the Employee Expenses table. Click No to save changes.

Activity 2: CREATING A CROSSTAB QUERY; FINDING UNMATCHED AND DUPLICATE RECORDS

1 With **WEEmployees4** open, create a crosstab query that will summarize expenses by employee by quarter using the following information:
   a Use the Employee Expenses table to generate the crosstab query.
   b Display the employee numbers in rows.
   c Display the date in quarter intervals in columns.
   d Sum the expense amounts.
   e Name the query Expenses by Employee by Quarter.
2 Adjust column widths as necessary and then print the query results datasheet.
3 Close the Expenses by Employee by Quarter query, saving changes.
4 Use the Find Unmatched Query Wizard to compare the Employees table with the Employee Expenses table and produce a list of employees who have not submitted an expense claim. Display the fields *Emp No, FirstName,* and *LastName* in the query results. Accept the default name for the query.
5 Print the query results datasheet.
6 Close the Employees Without Matching Employee Expenses query.
7 Use the Find Duplicates Query Wizard to analyze the *Emp No* field in the Employee Expenses table and produce a list of employees who have submitted more than one expense claim. Display the remaining three fields in the query results. Accept the default name for the query.
8 Print the query results datasheet.
9 Close the Find Duplicates for Employee Expenses query.

Activity 3: CREATING AND MODIFYING A REPORT; CREATING A CALCULATED CONTROL

1 With **WEEmployees4** open, create a new report using the Report Wizard based on the Trask Employee List query as follows:
  a Add all of the fields from the query to the report.
  b Do not include any grouping or sorting.
  c Select the *Columnar* layout.
  d Select the *Corporate* style.
  e Accept the default title for the report.
2 Display the Trask Employee List in Design view and then modify the report as follows:
  a Insert a label control in the *Report Header* section that will print the text *Report Design by: Student Name*. Substitute your first and last names for *Student Name*. Position the control near the right edge of the *Report Header* section and change the font size to 12-point. If necessary, resize the control after changing the font size. Select the report title and label control in the Report Header section and then use the Align Bottom option to position the bottom edges of both controls at the same horizontal position on the report.
  b Create a calculated control object to the right of the *Annual Salary* text box control that will calculate the monthly salary by dividing the Annual Salary by 12. Type the label **Monthly Salary** for the calculated control object.
  c Change the Format property for the calculated control object to *Currency*.
  d Use the Format Painter to copy the border style from the *Annual Salary* control object to the *Monthly Salary* control object.
  e Select the *Annual Salary* label and text box controls and the *Monthly Salary* label and text box controls. Use the Align Top option to make sure the controls are all at the same vertical position.
3 Save and then print the first page only of the report.
4 Close the Trask Employee List report.

Activity 4: CREATING A PIVOTTABLE

1 With **WEEmployees4** open, open the Trask Employee List query in Datasheet view.
2 Switch to PivotTable view.
3 Create a PivotTable that will summarize the annual salaries of employees by hire dates using the following information:
  a Drag the *Department* field to *Drop Filter Fields Here*.
  b Drag the *Last Name* field to *Drop Row Fields Here*.
  c Drag the *Hire Date By Month* field to *Drop Column Fields Here*.
  d Drag the *Annual Salary* field to *Drop Totals or Detail Fields Here*.
4 Close the PivotTable Field List box.
5 Filter the PivotTable on the Department field to display only those employees in the European Distribution and Overseas Distribution departments.
6 Filter the PivotTable on the Years field to display only those employees hired in the year 2000 and beyond.
7 Click any of the *Annual Salary* column headings. Turn on bold, change the font color to dark green, and choose a light green fill color.
8 Click the Save button and then print the PivotTable.
9 Close the Trask Employee List query.

Activity 5: CREATING A WEB PAGE; USING WEB PAGE PREVIEW

1 With **WEEmployees4** open, use the Page Wizard to create a Web page based on the Employee Dates and Salaries table as follows:
   - Add all of the fields except *Review Date* from the table to the Web page.
   - Do not include any grouping or sorting.
   - Accept the default title for the Web page.
2 Apply the *Compass* theme to the Web page.
3 Type **Worldwide Enterprises Dates and Salaries** as the title text in the Web page.
4 Save the Web page and name it **WEDatesAndSalaries**.
5 Display the Web page in the default browser window, and then view two or three records.
6 Print the Web page with the record expanded for employee number 1010.
7 Close the browser window.
8 Close the **WEDatesAndSalaries** Web page.
9 Close **WEEmployees4**.

PERFORMANCE PLUS

Assessment 1: MODIFYING A TABLE; APPLYING AND REMOVING A FILTER

1 After reviewing the inventory list with Dana Hirsch, manager of The Waterfront Bistro, you realize some adjustments need to be made to the structure of the table. Dana has also asked for a list of items that are purchased from supplier code 4.
2 Open **WBInventory4**.
3 Open the Inventory List table in Design view.
4 Make the following changes to the table:
   a Move the *Unit* field between the *Item No* and *Item* fields.
   b Move the *Supplier Code* field between the *Item No* and *Unit* fields.
5 Save the table and then switch to Datasheet view.
6 Turn on Filter By Form and then filter the records by *Supplier Code 4*.
7 Print the filtered datasheet and then remove the filter.
8 Close the Inventory List table. Click No to save changes.
9 Close the **WBInventory4** database.

Assessment 2: ADDING A CALCULATED CONTROL TO A FORM

1 Staff at Performance Threads have commented positively on the usefulness of the form created for browsing the inventory table. They have asked for a modification to the form that will allow them to tell customers what the daily rental fee is with the tax included.
2 Open **PTCostumeInventory4**.
3 Open the Costume Inventory form in Form view and review the current form layout and design.
4 Switch to Design view and then make the following changes:
   a Create a calculated control object to the right of the *Daily Rental Fee* object that will calculate the Daily Rental Fee with 7% GST included. (GST is the goods and services tax levied on all purchases by the government of Canada.)

    b Type **Rental fee tax included** as the label for the calculated control.

    c Format the calculated control object to *Currency.*

    d Use the Align Top option to make sure the calculated object is aligned horizontally with the top edge of the *Daily Rental Fee* object.

    e If necessary, resize the label and text box control to ensure the text and values are entirely visible.

    f Make sure the new object is the same font and font size as the other objects on the form.

    g Select all control objects within the *Detail* section of the form and increase vertical spacing twice. If necessary, drag the *Form Footer* section down to make more room in the *Detail* section.

5 Save the revised form and then switch to Form view.

6 Print the first record only in the form.

7 Close the form.

8 Close **PTCostumeInventory4**.

[handwritten: Total of Rental Fee + 7% tax]

Assessment 3: CREATING AND MODIFYING A REPORT

1 Heidi Pasqual, financial officer of Worldwide Enterprises, requires a report that will print the names and addresses of the Canadian distributors. Since Heidi is not familiar with Access, she has asked you to create the report for her.

2 Open **WEDistributors4**.

3 Create a new report using the Report Wizard as follows:

    • Select the *Name, Street Address1, Street Address2, City, Province,* and *Postal Code* fields from the Canadian Distributors table.

    • Do not include any grouping or sorting.

    • Choose the *Tabular* layout in *Portrait* orientation.

    • Choose the *Corporate* style.

    • Accept the default title of *Canadian Distributors.*

4 Preview the report at 100% magnification. Notice that some of the names and street addresses are truncated on the report.

5 Switch to Design view.

6 Resize and move the *City, Province,* and *Postal Code* controls in the *Page Header* and *Detail* sections to make enough room on the page to widen the name and address columns.

7 Widen the *Name, Street Address1,* and *Street Address2* controls in the *Page Header* and *Detail* sections.

8 View the report in Print Preview.

9 If necessary, switch to Design view and make further adjustments to the size and placement of the controls.

10 Select all of the control objects in the *Page Header* section and then use Align Top or Align Bottom to make sure all objects are at the same horizontal position.

11 Select all of the control objects in the *Detail* section and then use Align Top or Align Bottom to make sure all objects are at the same horizontal position.

12 Add a label object at the left side of the report in the *Report Footer* that includes the text *Report Design by: Student Name.* Substitute your first and last names for *Student Name.*

13 Save, print, and then close the Canadian Distributors Addresses report.

14 Close **WEDistributors4**.

Assessment 4: APPLYING AND REMOVING FILTERS

1   Niagara Peninsula College has received two student grants from Performance Threads to be awarded to the top two students in the Theatre Arts Division. Cal Rubine, chair of the Theatre Arts Division of Niagara Peninsula College, has requested a list of students who achieved A+ in a course for review by a selection committee.
2   Open **NPCGrades4**.
3   Open the ACT104 Grades table.
4   Filter the table to display only those records with an A+ in the *Grade* field.
5   Print and then close the table. Click No to save changes.
6   Open the PRD112 Grades table.
7   Filter the table to display only those records with an A+ in the *Grade* field.
8   Print and then close the table. Click No to save changes.
9   Open the SPE266 Grades table.
10 Filter the table to display only those records with an A+ in the *Grade* field.
11 Print and then close the table. Click No to save changes.
12 Close **NPCGrades4**.

Assessment 5: CREATING A PIVOTCHART

1   Dana Hirsch, manager of The Waterfront Bistro, is reviewing the recent purchases made by the executive chef and has requested a chart showing the dollar value of inventory purchases by item.
2   Open **WBInventory4**.
3   Create a new query in Design view as follows:
    • Add the Inventory List and Purchases tables to the design grid.
    • Add the fields in order: *Item No, Item, Unit, Supplier Code, Purchase Date, Amount*.
    • Name the query *Inventory Purchases*.
4   Run the query.
5   Switch to PivotChart view.
6   Create a PivotChart as follows:
    • Drag the *Supplier Code* field to *Drop Filter Fields Here*.
    • Drag the *Item* field to *Drop Category Fields Here*.
    • Drag the *Amount* field to *Drop Data Fields Here*.
7   Close the Chart Field List box.
8   Change the page orientation to landscape and then print the chart.
9   Filter the chart to display only those items purchased from Supplier Code 1.
10 Print the chart.
11 Redisplay all items in the chart.
12 Save and then close the Inventory Purchases query.

Assessment 6: CREATING AND MODIFYING A WEB PAGE

1 Dana Hirsch, manager of The Waterfront Bistro, has been considering posting the inventory purchases information on the company intranet for the executive chef, who is more familiar with Web browser navigation methods than Access. Dana has asked you to create a Web page from the Purchases table.

2 With **WBInventory4** open, create a Web page using the Page Wizard adding all fields from the Purchases table. Accept all other default settings in the Page Wizard dialog boxes.

3 Apply a theme of your choosing to the Web page.

4 Type **The Waterfront Bistro Inventory Purchases** as the title of the page.

5 Save the Web page and name it *InventoryPurchases*.

6 View the Web page in the Web browser window.

7 Scroll through and expand a few records in the Web browser window.

8 Switch back to Design view and move and resize controls as necessary so that all labels and field values are entirely visible.

9 Save the revised Web page and display Web Page Preview.

10 Scroll to record 5, expand the record, and then print the Web page from the browser window.

11 Close the Web browser window.

12 Close the InventoryPurchases Web page.

13 Close **WBInventory4**.

Assessment 7: FINDING INFORMATION ON ADDING FIELDS TO AN EXISTING REPORT

1 Use the Help feature to find out how to add a field to an existing report in Design view. *(Hint: A control that displays data from the associated table is considered a bound control.)*

2 Print the Help topic that you find.

3 Open **WEDistributors4**.

4 Open the Canadian Distributors Addresses report in Design view.

5 Change the page orientation to landscape and then drag the right edge of the design grid to position 8 on the horizontal ruler.

6 Add the *Telephone* field to the report. *(Hint: Cut and paste the label control for the* **Telephone** *field from the* **Detail** *section to the* **Page Header** *section after you have added the field. You may have to edit the control after it is pasted.)*

7 Adjust the length of the lines below the *Page Header* and above the *Page Footer* objects. Drag the page numbering control in the *Page Footer* section to the right edge of the report.

8 Preview the report.

9 Save, print, and then close the Canadian Distributors report.

10 Close **WEDistributors4**.

Assessment 8: RESEARCHING MOVIES ON THE INTERNET

1 Choose four movies that are currently playing in your vicinity that you have seen or would like to see, and then find their Web sites on the Internet. Look for the information listed in Step 3 that you will be entering into a new database.

2 Create a new database named **Movies**.

3 Create a table named Movie Facts that will store the following information:

Movie title   Lead actor—female
Director's name   Supporting actor—female
Producer's name   Movie category—drama, action, thriller, and so on
Lead actor—male   Web site address
Supporting actor—male

4 Design and create a form to enter the records for the movies you researched.

5 Enter the records using the form created in Step 4.

6 Print the last form only.

7 Design and create a report for the Movie Facts table. Add your name to the *Report Header* or *Report Footer* section in a label control object.

8 Print the Movie Facts report.

9 Close the **Movies** database.

INTEGRATED 2
Integrating Word, Excel, and Access

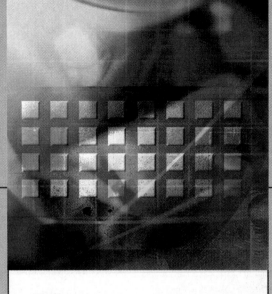

Data in one program within the Microsoft Office suite can be imported and/or exported to another program. For example, you can export data in an Access table to an Excel worksheet or a Word document. One of the advantages of exporting data to Excel or Word is that formatting can be applied using Excel or Word formatting features. You can also import data into an Access database file. If you know that you will update data in a program other than Access, link the data. Changes made to linked data are reflected in both the source and destination programs. In this section, you will learn the following skills and complete the projects described here.

 Note: The database files for this section are in the Integrated02 subfolder in the Integrated folder on the CD that accompanies this textbook. Before beginning this section, delete any existing databases on your disk and copy each database as needed. Remember to remove the read-only attribute from each database after copying. If necessary, refer to page 1 for instructions on how to remove the read-only attribute. If necessary, check with your instructor before deleting any database files.

Skills
- Export Access data in a table to Excel
- Export Access data in a table to Word
- Export Access data in a report to Word
- Import Excel data to a new Access table
- Link data between an Excel worksheet and an Access table
- Edit linked data

Projects

 Export grades for PRD112 from an Access table to an Excel worksheet. Import grades for a Beginning Theatre class from an Excel worksheet into an Access database table. Link grades for TRA220 between an Excel worksheet and an Access database table.

 Export data on costume inventory from an Access table to an Excel worksheet. Export data on costume inventory from an Access report to a Word document. Import data on costume design hours from an Excel worksheet into an Access table.

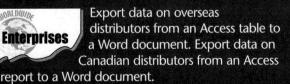 Export data on overseas distributors from an Access table to a Word document. Export data on Canadian distributors from an Access report to a Word document.

 Export data on inventory from an Access table to a Word document.

 Link data on booking commissions between an Excel worksheet and an Access table and then update the data.

I-2.1 Exporting Access Data to Excel

One of the advantages of a suite program like Microsoft Office is the ability to exchange data from one program to another. Access, like the other programs in the suite, offers a feature to export data from Access into Excel and/or Word. Export data using the OfficeLinks button on the Database toolbar. You can export Access data saved in a table, form, or report to Excel. The data is saved as an Excel file in the folder where Access is installed.

PROJECT: You are Katherine Lamont, Theatre Arts Division instructor at Niagara Peninsula College. You want to work on your grades for your PRD112 class over the weekend and you do not have Access installed on your personal laptop. You decide to export your Access grading table to Excel.

STEPS

1. Open Access and then open the **NPCClasses** database file. (Remove the read-only attribute.)

2. Click the Tables button on the Objects bar and then click once on *PRD112Grades* in the list box.

3. Click the down-pointing arrow at the right side of the OfficeLinks button on the Database toolbar.

4. At the drop-down list that displays, click *Analyze It with Microsoft Office Excel*.

5. When the data displays on the screen in Excel as a worksheet, insert the following grades in the specified cells:

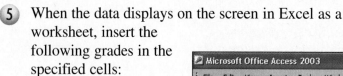

D2	=	B
D5	=	A
D13	=	D
D15	=	C
D16	=	D
D17	=	B

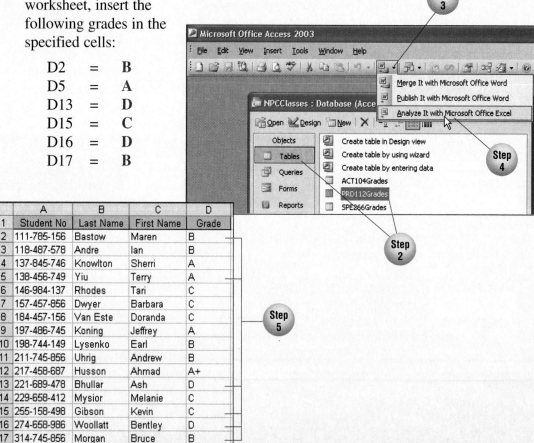

	A	B	C	D
1	Student No	Last Name	First Name	Grade
2	111-785-156	Bastow	Maren	B
3	118-487-578	Andre	Ian	B
4	137-845-746	Knowlton	Sherri	A
5	138-456-749	Yiu	Terry	A
6	146-984-137	Rhodes	Tari	C
7	157-457-856	Dwyer	Barbara	C
8	184-457-156	Van Este	Doranda	C
9	197-486-745	Koning	Jeffrey	A
10	198-744-149	Lysenko	Earl	B
11	211-745-856	Uhrig	Andrew	B
12	217-458-687	Husson	Ahmad	A+
13	221-689-478	Bhullar	Ash	D
14	229-658-412	Mysior	Melanie	C
15	255-158-498	Gibson	Kevin	C
16	274-658-986	Woollatt	Bentley	D
17	314-745-856	Morgan	Bruce	B

⑥ Select cells A1 through D17.

⑦ Click Format and then AutoFormat.

⑧ At the AutoFormat dialog box, scroll down the list of autoformats until *List 1* is visible and then double-click *List 1*.

Step 8

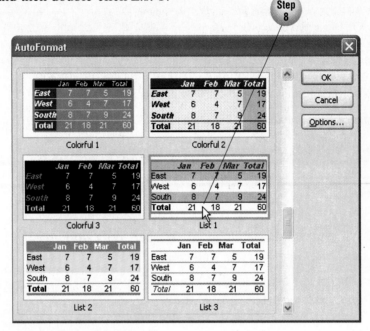

⑨ Deselect the cells by clicking outside the selected cells.

⑩ Save the worksheet with Save As and name it **IntE2-01**.

⑪ Print and then close **IntE2-01**.

⑫ Click the button on the Taskbar representing the Access database file **NPCClasses** and then close the database file.

In Addition

Exporting to Excel

Three methods are available for exporting Access data to an Excel worksheet. You can export data using the *Analyze It with Microsoft Office Excel* option from the OfficeLinks drop-down list as you did in this topic. You can save the output of a datasheet, form, or report directly as an Excel *(.xls)* worksheet or you can export the datasheet as unformatted data to Excel.

IN BRIEF

Export Access Table to Excel
1 Open database file.
2 Click Tables button on Objects bar and then click desired table.
3 Click down-pointing arrow at right side of OfficeLinks button.
4 Click *Analyze It with Microsoft Office Excel*.

I-2.2 Exporting Access Data to Word

Export data from Access to Word in the same manner as exporting to Excel. To export data to Word, open the database file, select the table, form, or report, and then click the OfficeLinks button on the Database toolbar. At the drop-down list, click *Publish It with Microsoft Office Word.* Word automatically opens and the data displays in a Word document that is automatically saved with the same name as the database table, form, or report. The difference is that the file extension *.rtf* is added to the name rather than the Word file extension *.doc.* An rtf file is saved in "rich-text

format," which preserves formatting such as fonts and styles. You can export a document saved with the *.rtf* extension in Word and other Windows word processing or desktop publishing programs.

***

PROJECT: Roman Deptulski, the manager of overseas distribution for Worldwide Enterprises, has asked you to export an Access database table containing information on overseas distributors to a Word document. He needs some of the information for a distribution meeting.

S T E P S

1. With Access the active program, open **WECompany**.

2. Click the Tables button on the Objects bar and then click once on *OverseasDistributors* in the list box.

3. Click the down-pointing arrow at the right side of the OfficeLinks button on the Database toolbar and then click *Publish It with Microsoft Office Word* at the drop-down list.

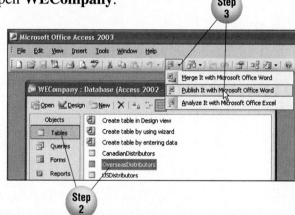

4. When the data displays on the screen in Word, select all of the cells in the two *Street* columns.

5. Delete the selected columns by clicking Table, pointing to Delete, and then clicking Columns.

6. Select all of the cells in the *Postal Code, Telephone,* and *Fax* columns, click Table, point to Delete, and then click Columns.

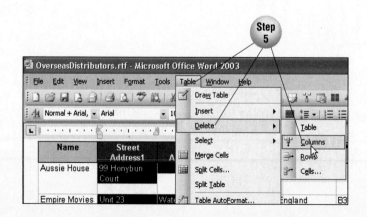

⑦ The Word Table feature has an autofit feature that will automatically adjust the column widths to the contents of the columns. Make sure the insertion point is positioned in a cell in the table and then use this feature by clicking Table, pointing to AutoFit, and then clicking AutoFit to Contents.

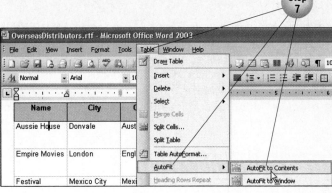

Step 7

⑧ With the insertion point positioned in any cell in the table, click Table and then Table AutoFormat.

⑨ At the Table AutoFormat dialog box, double-click *Table List 7* in the *Table styles* list box.

⑩ Click the Save button 🖫 to save the document with the same name (**OverseasDistributors**).

⑪ Print and then close **OverseasDistributors**.

⑫ Click the button on the Taskbar representing the **WECompany** Access database file and then close the database file.

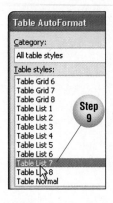

Step 9

In Addition

Adjusting a Table

In this section, you adjusted the Word table to the cell contents. The Table AutoFit feature contains several options for adjusting table contents. These options are:

Option	Action
AutoFit to Contents	Adjusts table to accommodate the table text
AutoFit to Window	Resizes table to fit within the window or browser. If browser changes size, table size automatically adjusts to fit within window
Fixed Column Width	Adjusts each column to a fixed width using the current widths of the columns
Distribute Rows Evenly	Changes selected rows or cells to equal row height
Distribute Columns Evenly	Changes selected columns or cells to equal column width

In BRIEF

Export Access Table to Word
1 Open database file.
2 Click Tables button on Objects bar and then click desired table.
3 Click down-pointing arrow at right side of OfficeLinks button.
4 Click *Publish It with Microsoft Office Word.*

I-2.3 Exporting an Access Report to Word

An Access report, like an Access table, can be exported to a Word document. Export a report to Word by using the *Publish It with Microsoft Office Word* option from the OfficeLinks drop-down list. One of the advantages to exporting a report to Word is that formatting can be applied to the report using Word formatting features.

PROJECT: Sam Vestering, manager of North American distribution for Worldwide Enterprises, needs a list of Canadian distributors. He has asked you to export a report to Word and then apply specific formatting to the report. He needs some of the information for a contact list.

S T E P S

1. With Access the active program, open **WECompany**.

2. At the WECompany : Database window, click the Reports button on the Objects bar.

3. Click *CanadianDistributorsAddresses* in the list box.

4. Click the down-pointing arrow at the right side of the OfficeLinks button and then click *Publish It with Microsoft Office Word*.

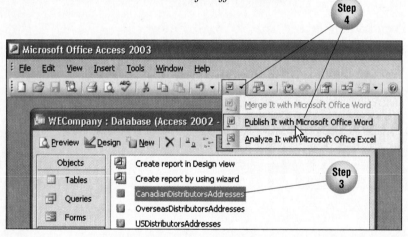

5. When the data displays on the screen in Word, press Ctrl + A to select the entire document.

6. Click the down-pointing arrow at the right side of the Font button on the Formatting toolbar and then click *Arial* at the drop-down list.

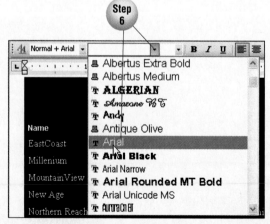

⑦ With the document still selected, click the down-pointing arrow at the right side of the Font Size button on the Formatting toolbar and then click *10* at the drop-down list.

⑧ Press Ctrl + Home to move the insertion point to the beginning of the document and then type **Worldwide Enterprises**.

⑨ Press Enter and then type **Canadian Distributors**.

⑩ Select *Worldwide Enterprises* and then change the font to 22-point Arial bold.

⑪ Select *Canadian Distributors* and then change the font to 18-point Arial bold.

⑫ Click the Save button 🖫 to save the report with the default name (**CanadianDistributorsAddresses**).

⑬ Print and then close **CanadianDistributorsAddresses**.

> The **CanadianDistributorsAddresses** document prints in landscape orientation and includes a footer at the bottom of the page that prints the current date.

⑭ Exit Word.

⑮ In Access, close the **WECompany** Access database file.

In Addition

Merging Access Data with a Word Document

Word includes a mail merge feature that you can use to create letters and envelopes and much more, with personalized information. Generally, a merge requires two documents—the *data source* and the *main document*. The data source contains the variable information that will be inserted in the main document. Create a data source document in Word or create a data source using data from an Access table. When merging Access data, you can either type the text in the main document or merge Access data with an existing Word document. To merge data in an Access table, open the database file, click the Tables button on the Objects bar, and then click the desired table. Click the OfficeLinks button on the Database toolbar and then click Merge It with Microsoft Office Word. Follow the steps presented in the Mail Merge task pane to complete the merge.

In Brief

Export Access Report to Word
1 Open database file.
2 Click Reports button on Objects bar and then click desired report.
3 Click down-pointing arrow at right side of OfficeLinks button.
4 Click *Publish It with Microsoft Office Word*.

I-2.4 Importing Data to a New Table

In the previous three topics, you exported Access data to Excel and Word. You can also import data from other programs into an Access table. For example, you can import data from an Excel worksheet and create a new table in a database file. Data in the original program is not connected to the data imported into an Access table. If you make changes to the data in the original program, those changes are not reflected in the Access table.

PROJECT: You are Gina Simmons, Theatre Arts instructor, and have recorded grades in an Excel worksheet for your students in the Beginning Theatre class. You want to import those grades into the NPCClasses database file.

S T E P S

1. In Access, open the **NPCClasses** database file and then click the Tables button on the Objects bar.

2. Import an Excel worksheet by clicking File, pointing to Get External Data, and then clicking Import.

3. At the Import dialog box, change the *Files of type* option to *Microsoft Excel*, and then double-click **NPCBegThGrades** in the list box.

   Your list of documents may vary from what you see in the image below and at the right.

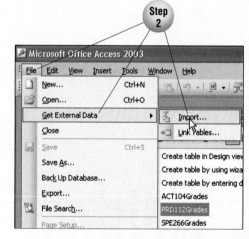

PROBLEM ?
If *NPCBegThGrades* does not display in the list box, you may need to navigate to another folder. Check with your instructor.

4. At the first Import Spreadsheet Wizard dialog box, click the Next button.

5. At the second dialog box, insert a check mark in the *First Row Contains Column Headings* option and then click the Next button.

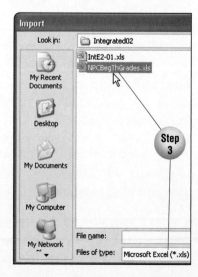

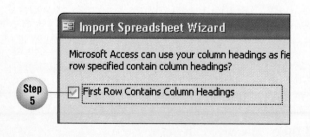

⑥ At the third dialog box, make sure the *In a New Table* option is selected and then click the Next button.

⑦ At the fourth dialog box, click the Next button.

⑧ At the fifth dialog box, click the *Choose my own primary key* option (this inserts *Student No* in the text box located to the right of the option), and then click the Next button.

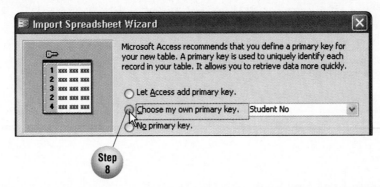

Step 8

⑨ At the sixth dialog box, type **BegThGrades** in the *Import to Table* text box and then click the Finish button.

⑩ At the message saying the data was imported, click OK.

⑪ Open the new table by double-clicking **BegThGrades** in the list box.

⑫ Print and then close **BegThGrades**.

⑬ Close the **NPCClasses** database file.

Step 9

In Addition

Importing or Linking a Table

You can import data from another program into an Access table or you can link the data. Choose the method depending on how you are going to use the data. Import data to a table if you are going to use the data only in Access. Access generally operates faster working with its own tables. Link data to an Access table if the data will be changed or updated in a program other than Access. Changes made to linked data are reflected in both the source and destination programs.

In BRIEF

Import Data to a New Table
1 Open database file.
2 Click Tables button on Objects bar.
3 Click File, Get External Data, Import.
4 Follow the Import Wizard steps.

I-2.5 Linking Data to a New Table and Editing Linked Data

Imported data is not connected to the source program. If you know that you will use your data only in Access, import it. However, if you want to update data in a program other than Access, link the data. Changes made to linked data are reflected in both the source and destination programs. For example, you can link an Excel worksheet with an Access table and when you make changes in either the Excel worksheet or the Access table, the change is reflected in the other program. To link data to a new table, open the database file, click File, point to Get External Data, and then click Link Tables. At the Link dialog box, double-click the desired document name. This activates the link wizard that walks you through the steps to link the data.

PROJECT: You are Gina Simmons, Theatre Arts instructor at Niagara Peninsula College. You record students' grades in an Excel worksheet and also link the grades to an Access database file. With the data linked, changes you make to either the Excel table or the Access table will be reflected in the other table.

STEPS

1. Open Excel and then open **NPCTRA220**.

2. Save the worksheet with Save As and name it **IntE2-02**.

3. Print and then close **IntE2-02**.

4. Make Access the active program, open the **NPCClasses** database file, and then click the Tables button on the Objects bar.

5. Link an Excel worksheet by clicking File, pointing to Get External Data, and then clicking Link Tables.

Step 5

6. At the Link dialog box, change the *Files of type* option to *Microsoft Excel* and then double-click *IntE2-02* in the list box.

   Depending on your system configuration, you may need to navigate to the folder containing **IntE2-02**.

7 At the first Link Spreadsheet Wizard dialog box, make sure *Show Worksheets* is selected, and that *Sheet1* is selected in the list box, and then click the Next button.

8 At the second dialog box, make sure the *First Row Contains Column Headings* option contains a check mark and then click the Next button.

Step 7

Link Spreadsheet Wizard

Your spreadsheet file contains more than one would you like?

◉ Show Worksheets
○ Show Named Ranges

Sheet1
Sheet2
Sheet3

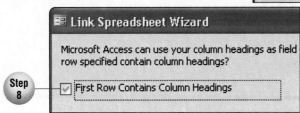

Link Spreadsheet Wizard

Microsoft Access can use your column headings as field row specified contain column headings?

Step 8

☑ First Row Contains Column Headings

9 At the third dialog box, type **LinkedGrades** in the *Linked Table Name* text box, and then click the Finish button.

10 At the message stating the link is finished, click OK.

Access uses different icons to represent linked tables and tables that are stored in the current database. Notice the icon that displays before the LinkedGrades table.

Link Spreadsheet Wizard

That's all the information the wizard needs to

Linked Table Name:

LinkedGrades

Step 9

11 Open the new LinkedGrades table in Datasheet view.

12 As you look at the table, you realize that you need to add a student to the end of the list. Add the following new record in the specified fields (see image below):

Student No	Student	Midterm
138-456-749	Yui, T.	3.25

LinkedGrades : Table

	Student No	Student	Midterm	Final
	111-75-156	Bastow, M.	3.25	
	359-845-475	Collyer, S.	1.50	
	157-457-856	Dwyer, B.	3.50	
	348-876-486	Ennis, A.	2.25	
	378-159-746	Gagne, M.	3.00	
	197-486-745	Koning, J.	2.75	
	314-745-856	Morgan, B.	3.75	
	349-874-658	Retieffe, S.	4.00	
𝐼	138-456-749	Yui, T.	3.25	
*				

Step 12

(continued)

(13) Print and then close the LinkedGrades table.

The new record is automatically saved when the table is closed.

(14) Make Excel the active program and then open **IntE2-02**.

Notice that the worksheet contains the student, Yui, T., you added to the Access table.

(15) You have finished grading student finals and need to insert the grades in the worksheet. Insert the following grades in the specified cells:

D2 = 2.75
D3 = 1
D4 = 3.5
D5 = 2
D6 = 3.5
D7 = 2.5
D8 = 3
D9 = 3.5
D10 = 2.5

	A	B	C	D
1	Student No	Student	Midterm	Final
2	111-75-156	Bastow, M.	3.25	2.75
3	359-845-475	Collyer, S.	1.50	1.00
4	157-457-856	Dwyer, B.	3.50	3.50
5	348-876-486	Ennis, A.	2.25	2.00
6	378-159-746	Gagne, M.	3.00	3.50
7	197-486-745	Koning, J.	2.75	2.50
8	314-745-856	Morgan, B.	3.75	3.00
9	349-874-658	Retieffe, S.	4.00	3.50
10	138-456-749	Yui, T.	3.25	2.50

Step 15

(16) Make cell E2 the active cell and then insert a formula to average scores by clicking the Insert Function button f_x on the Formula bar.

(17) At the Insert Function dialog box, double-click *AVERAGE* in the *Select a function* list box.

PROBLEM?

If AVERAGE is not visible in the *Select a function* list box, click the down-pointing arrow at the right side of the *Or select a category* option box, and then click *Most Recently Used* at the drop-down list.

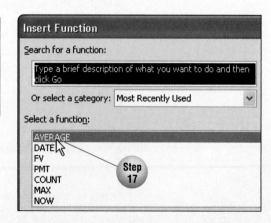

Insert Function

Search for a function:

Type a brief description of what you want to do and then click Go

Or select a category: Most Recently Used

Select a function:

AVERAGE
DATE
FV
PMT
COUNT
MAX
NOW

Step 17

18 At the formula palette, make sure *C2:D2* displays in the Number1 text box and then click OK.

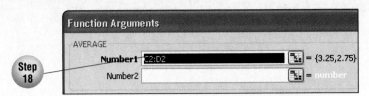

Step 18

Function Arguments		
AVERAGE		
Number1	C2:D2	= {3.25,2.75}
Number2		= number

19 Using the fill handle, copy the formula down to cell E10.

	A	B	C	D	E
1	Student No	Student	Midterm	Final	Average
2	111-75-156	Bastow, M.	3.25	2.75	3.00
3	359-845-475	Collyer, S.	1.50	1.00	1.25
4	157-457-856	Dwyer, B.	3.50	3.50	3.50
5	348-876-486	Ennis, A.	2.25	2.00	2.13
6	378-159-746	Gagne, M.	3.00	3.50	3.25
7	197-486-745	Koning, J.	2.75	2.50	2.63
8	314-745-856	Morgan, B.	3.75	3.00	3.38
9	349-874-658	Retieffe, S.	4.00	3.50	3.75
10	138-456-749	Yui, T.	3.25	2.50	2.88
11					

Step 19

20 Deselect the cells by clicking outside the selected cells.

21 Save and then print **IntE2-02**.

22 Click the button on the Taskbar representing the **NPCClasses** Access database file.

23 Open the LinkedGrades table.

> Notice that this linked table contains the final grades and the average scores you inserted in the Excel **IntE2-02** worksheet.

24 Print and then close the LinkedGrades table.

25 Close the **NPCClasses** database file and then close Access.

26 With Excel the active program, close **IntE2-02** and then close Excel.

In Addition

Deleting the Link to a Linked Table

If you want to delete the link to a table, open the database file, and then click the Tables button on the Objects bar. Click the linked table in the list box and then click the Delete button on the Tables toolbar (or press the Delete key). At the Microsoft question asking if you want to remove the link to the table, click Yes. Access deletes the link and removes the table's name from the list box. When you delete a linked table, you are deleting the information Access uses to open the table, not the table itself. You can link to the same table again, if necessary.

In Brief

Link Data to a New Table
1 Open database file.
2 Click Tables button on Objects bar.
3 Click File, Get External Data, Link Tables.
4 Follow the Link Wizard steps.

SKILLS REVIEW

Activity 1: EXPORTING ACCESS DATA TO EXCEL

1 Open Access and then open the **PTCostumes** database file.
2 Click the Tables button on the Objects bar and then export the data in the CostumeInventory table to Excel.
3 When the data displays in Excel, make the following changes in the specified cells:

     C4   =   Change *110.00* to *120.00*
     C5   =   Change *110.00* to *125.00*
     C7   =   Change *99.50* to *105.00*

4 Select cells A1 through E17 and then apply an autoformat of your choosing.
5 Save the worksheet with Save As and name it **IntE2-R1**.
6 Print and then close **IntE2-R1**.
7 Click the button on the Taskbar representing the Access database file **PTCostumes** and then close the database file.

Activity 2: EXPORTING ACCESS DATA TO WORD

1 With Access the active program, open **WBSupplies**.
2 Click the Tables button on the Objects bar and then export the data in the InventoryList table to Word.
3 When the data displays on the screen in Word, apply a table autoformat of your choosing to the table.
4 Move the insertion point to the beginning of the document, press Enter three times, and then move the insertion point back to the beginning of the document.
5 Type **The Waterfront Bistro** on the first line and type **Inventory List** on the second line.
6 Select *The Waterfront Bistro* and *Inventory List* and then change the font to 22-point Arial bold.
7 Save the Word document with the default name (**InventoryList**).
8 Print and then close **InventoryList**.
9 Click the button on the Taskbar representing the Access database file **WBSupplies** and then close the database file.

Activity 3: EXPORTING AN ACCESS REPORT TO WORD

1 With Access the active program, open **PTCostumes**.
2 At the PTCostumes Database window, click the Reports button on the Objects bar and then export the CostumeInventory report to a Word document.
3 When the data displays on the screen in Word, move the insertion point to the beginning of the document and then type **Performance Threads**.
4 Press the Enter key and then type **Costume Inventory**.
5 Increase the size and apply bolding to *Performance Threads* and *Costume Inventory*.
6 Save the Word document with the default name (**CostumeInventory**).
7 Print and then close **CostumeInventory**.
8 Exit Word.
9 With Access the active program, close the **PTCostumes** database file.

Activity 4: IMPORTING DATA TO A NEW TABLE

1 In Access, open the **PTCostumes** database file and then click the Tables button on the Objects bar.
2 Import the Excel worksheet named **PTCostumeHours**. (Make sure you change the *Files of type* option to *Microsoft Excel (*.xls),* and then double-click ***PTCostumeHours*** in the list box. Do not make any changes to the first Import Spreadsheet Wizard dialog box. At the second dialog box, make sure the *First Row Contains Column Headings* option contains a check mark. Make sure the *In a New Table* option is selected at the third dialog box. Do not make changes to the fourth dialog box and click the *No Primary key* option at the fifth dialog box. At the sixth dialog box, type **DesignHours** in the *Import to Table* text box, and then click the Finish button.)
3 Open the new DesignHours table.
4 Print and then close the DesignHours table.
5 Close the **PTCostumes** database file.

Activity 5: LINKING DATA TO A NEW TABLE AND EDITING LINKED DATA

1 Open Excel and then open **FCTBookings**.
2 Save the worksheet with Save As and name it **IntE2-R2**.
3 Make Access the active program, open the **FCTCommissions** database file, and then click the Tables button on the Objects bar.
4 Link the Excel worksheet **IntE2-R2** with the **FCTCommissions** database file. (At the Link dialog box, make sure you change the *Files of type* option to *Microsoft Excel*. At the third Link Spreadsheet Wizard dialog box, type **LinkedCommissions** in the *Linked Table Name* text box.)
5 Open, print, and then close the new LinkedCommissions table.
6 Click the button on the Taskbar representing the Excel worksheet **IntE2-R2**.
7 Make cell C2 active and then type the formula =B2*0.03 and then press Enter.
8 Make cell C2 active and then use the fill handle to copy the formula down to cell C13.
9 Save, print, and then close **IntE2-R2**.
10 Click the button on the Taskbar representing the **FCTCommissions** Access database file and then open the LinkedCommissions table.
11 Save, print, and then close the LinkedCommissions table.
12 Close the **FCTCommissions** database file.
13 Exit Access and then exit Excel.